Stitching a Legacy

Stitching *a* Legacy

AMERICAN NEEDLEWORK
PROJECTS AND STORIES

PieceWork Magazine in Association with the Peabody Essex Museum

FOREWORD BY PAULA BRADSTREET RICHTER

PROJECTS DESIGNED BY ANN CASWELL

 INTERWEAVE PRESS

Editor: Jeane Hutchins
Copy Editor: Betsy Strauch
Technical Editor: Dorothy T. Ratigan
Contributing Editor: Judith Durant
Editorial Director: Marilyn Murphy
Production: Dean Howes
Project Photo Stylist: Susan Strawn Bailey
Project Photographer: Joe Coca

Front Cover Photograph Copyright © 2001 Peabody Essex Museum
Front Cover Photograph by Jeffrey Dykes
Front Cover Design by Susan Wasinger
Back Cover Design by Jason Reid
Back Cover Photographs Copyright © 2001 Interweave Press and Joe Coca
Back Cover Photographs by Joe Coca
Page Design by Jason Reid and Dean Howes

Interweave Press
201 East Fourth Street
Loveland, Colorado 80537
www.interweave.com

Printed in Canada

Library of Congress Cataloging-in-Publication Data

Stitching a legacy : American needlework projects and stories / foreword by Paula
Bradstreet Richter ; [editor, Jeane Hutchins].
    p. cm.
  Needlework projects drawn from pieces in the needlework collection of the Peabody
Essex Museum and translated into fashion, home accessories, and heirloom keepsakes.
  ISBN 1-883010-90-X
  1.Needlework-Patterns.2.Needlework-United States-History.3.
  Neddlework-Catalogs and collections-Massachusetts-Salem.4.Peabody Essex
  Museum. I.Hutchins, Jeane, 1947-

TT751 .S75 2001
746.44'041'0973-dc21   2001016835

IWP:5M:201:FP

Foreword

Americans have practiced the ancient art of embroidery since the earliest days of colonial settlement. Whether worked on a schoolgirl's sampler, an eighteenth-century gentleman's waistcoat, a baby's christening dress, or a colonial governor's gloves, embroidery indicates its maker's intent to create an object that is not only useful but beautiful as well. A needleworker of outstanding vision and skill can produce embroidery that resonates with personal and/or cultural meanings comparable to those shown by other artistic media.

It is a pleasure to welcome you to *Stitching a Legacy: American Needlework Projects and Stories,* a collaborative venture by PIECE-WORK magazine and the Peabody Essex Museum of Salem, Massachusetts. This book contains two dozen needlework projects adapted from examples of needlework in the museum's collections. Profiles of the original embroiders place them in their historic and artistic

The Peabody Essex Museum in Salem, Massachusetts.

context, and clear instructions guide you in making the projects.

Founded in 1799, the Peabody Essex Museum, located north of Boston on the Atlantic coast of Massachusetts, is the country's oldest continuously operated museum. Its founders were bold seafaring entrepreneurs who sailed across uncharted oceans to China, Japan, India, Africa, the Pacific Islands, and the northwestern coast of North America. They established the museum to house and display not only the art and artifacts that they had acquired in distant ports but also objects from New England. In addition to its thirty galleries of collections, the museum also offers historic houses and gardens and a research library as well as lectures, special events, and educational programs. The facilities are being expanded to permit the display of an even greater part of the collection.

The American Decorative Arts Department contains more than 25,000 textiles, including samplers, garments, and household furnishings, as well as needlework tools. Other departments house textile collections representing Asian export, Chinese, Japanese, South East Asian, African, Native American, Pacific, and maritime art.

The publication of *Stitching a Legacy* celebrates the opening, on April 13, 2001, of "Painted with Thread: The Art of American Embroidery," an exhibition of about one hundred works from the museum's collections that were made or used in America from the seventeenth century to the present day. Among them are the twenty-four embroideries that inspired the projects in this publication. The exhibition, which runs through September 2001, also includes twentieth-century artworks borrowed from private and institutional collections that demonstrate recent, dynamic uses of embroidery. An illustrated catalog of the exhibition is also available from the Museum Shop.

I hope the projects and stories that you encounter in the pages of *Stitching a Legacy* will inspire you to use embroidery to create your own needlework legacy.

Paula Bradstreet Richter
Curator of Costumes and Textiles
Peabody Essex Museum

Preface

In June 2000, Interweave Press received a call from the Peabody Essex Museum in Salem, Massachusetts, inquiring whether PIECEWORK magazine might be interested in collaborating on a major exhibition of needlework from the museum's permanent collection. "Painted with Thread: The Art of American Embroidery" was to open April 13, 2001, and run through September 30. Two weeks later, Marilyn Murphy, our editorial director, and I met with members of the museum's staff and concluded that there were indeed opportunities for collaboration.

In July, I was again in Salem, this time to select the objects that would be in the exhibition to serve as inspiration for the projects to be featured in this book. The depth and breadth of the museum's needlework collection made this task both exciting and daunting—but choices were made. Now, all that remained was to get projects designed, stitched, photographed; get instructions written and edited; and get the book to the printer by mid-February 2001 so that the book would be out in time for the exhibition's opening in April. The results are in your hands.

In the following pages, you will find glimpses of the lives and times of some extraordinarily accomplished needleworkers. The people and their work span four centuries of American life from the early colonial period to the turn of the twentieth century; the earliest textiles are a pair of gloves worn in the 1600s, and the latest is an evening cape made between 1900 and 1905. Each story is accompanied by photographs of the object itself and the project or projects that it inspired. All of the projects have materials lists, instructions, charts, diagrams, or illustrations. A compendium of diagrams of the stitches used in the projects begins on page 116. A bibliography and contact information for the Embroiderers' Guild of America and the American Needlepoint Guild are found in the Resources section. Contact information for the suppliers of the materials used in the projects are in the Suppliers section.

Many people helped make this book possible. Sincere thanks to members of the American Needlepoint Guild, Inc., and the Embroiderers' Guild of America, Inc. (listed below), for stitching the projects so beautifully under an almost-impossible deadline and to members of both organizations for their information and advice; to Paula Richter, curator of textiles and costumes, and Kristen Weiss, collections manager, at the Peabody Essex Museum, for their time and expertise; to Julianna Mahley for encouragement; to Jean Campbell for advice on beading; and to Jake Rexus, Judy Kettner, Dee Lockwood, and Doree Pitkin for finishing some of the projects. Above all, my deepest gratitude goes to the stitchers of the original pieces, without whose legacy we would not have this book.

Jeane Hutchins
Editor
PIECEWORK Magazine

THE STITCHERS

American Needlepoint Guild: Penny Boswinkle, Dunwoody, Georgia; LaMona Brown, Washington, Missouri; Mary K. Campbell, Omaha, Nebraska; Vicki Coleman, Houston, Texas; Pamela Harding, North Bend, Washington; Lee McLeron, Spokane, Washington; Donna Neilson, Honolulu, Hawaii; Neva Pruess, Lincoln, Nebraska; John Savage, Atlanta, Georgia; and Barbara Smith, Chesterfield, Missouri. Embroiderers' Guild of America: Kay Griffith, Defiance, Ohio; Carol Higginbotham, Alhambra, California; Anne Holly, San Francisco, California; Judy Jeroy, Virginia Beach, Virginia; Jeanette Lovensheimer, Florence, South Carolina; Lynda Patterson, San Francisco, California; Angeline Shuh, Davenport, Iowa; Diana Snyder, South Burlington, Vermont; Carolyn Webb, Salt Lake City, Utah; and Kathy Weigl, Carlisle, Pennsylvania.

Contents

Portrait of Eunice Brown Fitch (1731–1799) by Joseph Blackburn. American. Oil on canvas. After 1760.

48½ × 39½ inches (123.2 × 100.3 cm). (1962).

Governor Leverett's Gloves

Gloves are among the most ancient and also most enduring fashion accessories. Linen gloves were found in the tomb of Egyptian king Tutankhamen (circa 1370–1352 B.C.), medieval European nobles wore both fabric and leather

Gloves. Maker unknown. Silk and metallic threads and spangles on leather. England. 1640–1660. 12¾ × 7 inches (32.4 × 17.8 cm). (106845).

gloves that were often richly bejeweled, Catherine de Médicis (1519–1589) made gloves a woman's fashion in sixteenth-century France, and glove making became an industry in the 1830s. Today, gloves are made by machine from high-tech fabrics in many styles for sport and warmth, and they are also a favorite project among handknitters.

Gloves were important ceremonial accessories in seventeenth-century England and colonial America: exchanged between monarchs and members of the nobility as symbols of loyalty, given by families at weddings and betrothals to seal covenants, and worn by cavaliers as tokens of love and devotion. Some gloves bore emblems having specific significance or purposes.

The elaborately embroidered leather gloves shown here probably were professionally embroidered in London, England, and they belonged to the prominent merchant, military leader, and governor of the Massachusetts Bay Colony John Leverett (1616–1679). Leverett lived in England between 1655 and 1661 and may have bought the gloves there, or he may have purchased them in Boston. Sumptuary laws of the period dictated that clothing be appropriate to the estate and quality of the wearer, and the silk, metallic gold and silver thread, and spangles (circular pieces of metal) that adorn this pair certainly made them suitable to a person of great importance.

A POCKET FLAP FOR A BLAZER TO EMBROIDER AND BEAD

A POCKET FLAP FOR A BLAZER
TO EMBROIDER AND BEAD

A motif stitched in silk and metallic threads with small gold and silver beads embellishes this insert for the breast pocket of a classic black wool blazer. A similar motif worked in gold and silver raised embroidery is a prominent feature on the pair of leather gloves worn in the 1600s by Massachusetts Bay Colony Governor John Leverett.

MATERIALS

Wool fabric, Black, 1 piece 6 × 6 inches (15.2 × 15.2 cm)

Interfacing, Black, 1 piece 3½ × 4¼ inches (8.9 × 10.8 cm)

Lining fabric, Black, 1 piece 5 × 5 inches (12.7 cm × 12.7 cm)

Kreinik Fine (#8) Braid, 11 yards (10 meters)/reel, 1 reel each in the colors listed in the Color Guide

Kreinik Petite Facets, multifaceted metallic thread, 5 meters (5.5 yards)/reel, 1 reel each in the colors listed in the Color Guide

Kreinik Japan #1 Threads, 40 meters (44 yards)/reel, 1 reel each in the colors listed in the Color Guide

Kreinik Silk Mori, 100% silk 6-strand thread, 5 meters (5.5 yards)/skein, 1 skein each in the colors listed in the Color Guide

SJ Designs galvanized beads, size 14, about 500 beads/packet, 1 packet each in the colors listed in the Color Guide

Needles, chenille size 14 (for sinking threads) and 18 (for satin stitch), embroidery size 9 (for couching), milliners size 9 (for bullion stitch), and sharps size 12 (for beading)

Sewing thread to match fabric (for finishing) and a contrasting color (for basting)

Embroidery hoop, small

Pencil, HB

Tissue paper

Finished size: Flap, 4½ × 3¾ inches (11.4 × 9.5 cm) opened; design size, 1½ × 3¾ inches (3.8 × 9.5 cm)

INSTRUCTIONS

The pocket flap is constructed so that the 1½-inch-high (3.8-cm) design is at the top of the 4½-inch (11.4-cm) piece of wool fabric. When the flap is inserted into the breast pocket of a blazer, the design area is folded down over the front of the pocket.

Trace the pattern onto the tissue paper. Center the tissue pattern on the right side of the wool fabric so that the bottom of the design is 2 inches (5.1 cm) from the top of the fabric (see illustration); pin. Center the fabric in the hoop. Using the sewing needle, baste the tissue onto the fabric with small stitches, following the traced lines. Tear off the tissue. Check the fabric to ensure that the entire design has been stitched.

Begin stitching at the top center of the design. All surrounding heavy gold lines (ovals and crescents) are gold Petite Facets couched with #002J and the size 9 embroidery needle. Sink the ends at each point using the size 14 chenille needle; couch with #002J and the size 9 embroidery needle. All surrounding heavy silver lines are silver Petite Facets couched with #001J. Sink the ends at each point; couch with #001J. All surrounding light gold lines (ovals and crescents) are #002C #8 Braid couched with #002J. Sink the ends at each point; couch with #002J.

All surrounding light silver lines are #001C #8 Braid couched with #001J. Sink the ends at each point; couch with #001J. Wind 12 inches (30.5 cm) of #205C #8 Braid into a spiral and couch with #002J. Sink the ends at each point; couch with #002J.

Work the heavy horizontal lines in bullion stitch, using the size 9 milliners needle and alternating #8084 and #2014 Silk Mori. Work the solid silver areas in padded satin stitch, using the size 18 chenille needle and #8084 Silk Mori. Fill in the designated areas randomly with silver and gold beads, using the size 12 sharps needle and matching (#001J or #002J) couching thread.

Remove the fabric from the hoop.

FINISHING

Interface the fabric according to the manufacturer's directions and pin the fabric to the lining fabric, right sides together. Allowing ½ inch (1.3 cm) for seams, sew around three sides, leaving an opening at the bottom. Trim the seams and clip the corners. Turn the flap right side out and slipstitch the lower edge closed. Fold over the top and tack the corners at the fold line to maintain the fold. Insert the flap into the pocket with the lining side facing forward so that the design is visible.

Pattern shown is actual size. Pattern may be photocopied for personal use.

Color Guide

Kreinik Fine (#8) Braid
001C—Silver

002C—Gold

205C—Antique Gold

Kreinik Petite Facets
Silver

Gold

Kreinik Silk Mori
Medium Gold—2014

Medium Gray—8084

SJ Designs Beads
1858— Gold

1859—Silver

Kreinik Japan #1 Threads

001J—Silver

002J—Gold

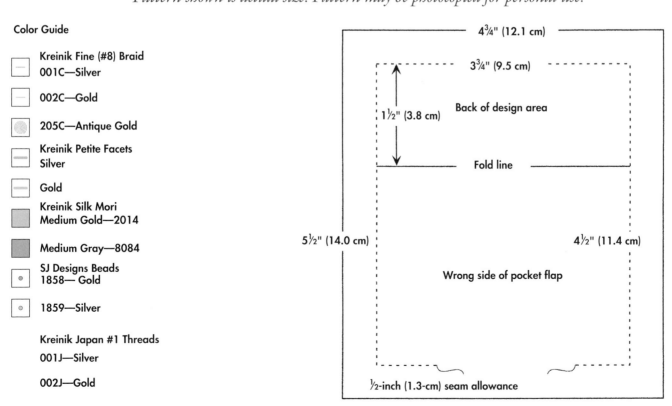

An Embroidered Treasure Chest

Embroidered cabinet; attributed to the daughters of Governor John Leverett. Silk and metallic threads on linen. New England or England. 1655–1685. 12 × 10⅞ × 7½ inches (30.5 × 27.6 × 19.1 cm). (118284).

An embroidered cabinet was the *pièce de résistance* on which a young woman might show her accomplishments with needle and thread, and she would undertake one only after having completed several types of samplers. Textile scholars believe materials and hand-drawn patterns for cabinets were sold as components in London and other European cities during the mid-seventeenth century.

This cabinet is believed to have been worked by one or more of the six daughters of Governor John Leverett. The Leveretts may have purchased the components for the cabinet during their stay in England from 1655 to 1661. Making a cabinet from components would only slightly reduce the amount of painstaking, and tedious work needed to execute a piece of this magnitude.

The cabinet, completed between 1655 and 1685, is made of silk, linen, metallic thread, wood, gilding, gesso, and brass. It was intended to hold valuables, including jewelry, pens and ink, needlework tools, or miniatures. The front panels depict the presentation of Queen Esther as chronicled in the Bible. Women from the Old Testament were role models and heroines to British and American young women during the seventeenth century, and they are popular subjects in the needlework produced in both countries. The sloping panel on the front of the lid showing a sailing vessel with two figures in a small boat rowing to shore may depict colonial migration or trans-Atlantic travel to New England. The cabinet's original wooden case is also in the museum's collection.

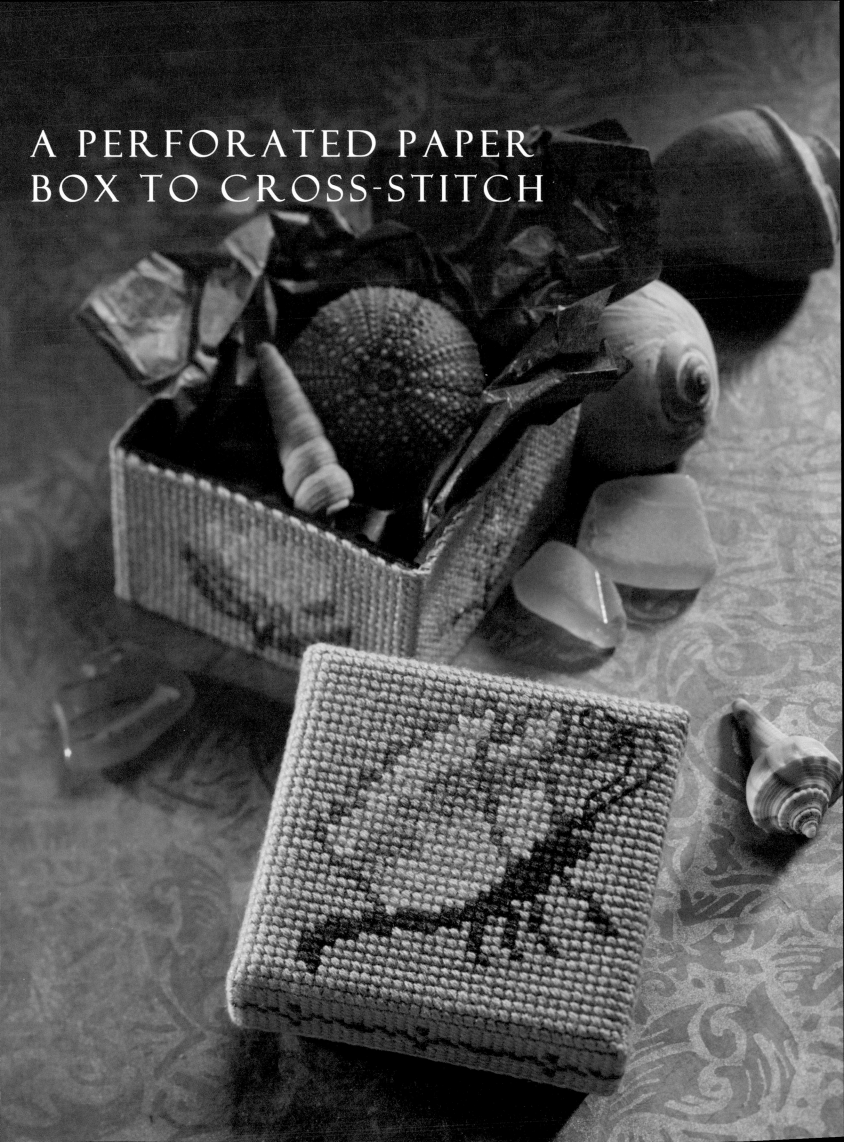

A PERFORATED PAPER
BOX TO CROSS-STITCH

A PERFORATED PAPER BOX TO CROSS-STITCH

Stitching an embroidered cabinet was a serious undertaking for a needleworker in the seventeenth century. Although the components could be purchased, a great deal of skill and untold hours were required to complete the project. Our cross-stitch-on-perforated-paper box uses motifs from an embroidered cabinet worked sometime between 1655 and 1685. A butterfly from the right side of the cabinet is worked on the top of the box, and several of the floral motifs are worked on the sides.

MATERIALS

Caron Collection Waterlilies, 100% hand-dyed silk, 12-strand thread, 6 yards (5.5 meters)/skein, 1 skein each in the colors listed in the Color Guide

Caron Collection Soie Cristale, 100% silk 12-strand thread, 6 yards (5.5 meters)/skein, 1 skein each in colors listed in the Color Guide

Needle, tapestry size 24

Perforated paper, Antique Brown, 1 sheet 9 x 12 inches (22.9 × 30.5 cm)

Matboard, Black, black core, 1 sheet 9 × 12 inches (22.9 × 30.5 cm)

Watercolor paper, heavy, 1 small sheet

Paintbrush, ½ inch (1.3 cm) wide

Aleene's Original Tacky Glue

Toothpicks

X-acto or mat knife with sharp blades

Metal straightedge

Pencil

Felt marker, black permanent

Finished size: 2½ × 2½ × 1½ inches (6.4 × 6.4 × 3.8 cm)

INSTRUCTIONS

Refer to the Stitch Diagrams on pages 116–119. Using the pencil, establish the center on the perforated paper. Using the tapestry needle and 3 strands of silk, cross-stitch the designs for the top and bottom of the box according to the charts. The areas shaded in gray will be stitched during finishing. Work the top of the box first. Begin stitching at the top of the design (marked on the chart) and work down, omitting the left and right sides for the moment. When the last row of stitching is complete, rotate the work 90 degrees and stitch downward from the previously stitched area toward the edge of the perforated paper. Stitch the other side in the same manner. Repeat for the bottom of the box. Trim beginning and ending thread ends to 1/4 inch (6 mm); secure them to the back of the work with a small amount of glue applied with a toothpick.

FINISHING

Cut and assemble the box following the finishing diagrams.

Box top

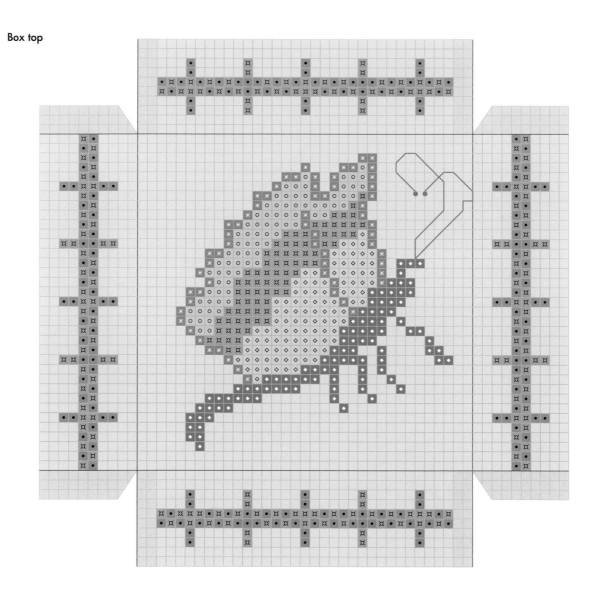

COLOR GUIDE

Waterlilies
| ¤ | 053—Coral Blush |

| ∷ | 066—Jade |

| ◇ | 094—Lemon Meringue |

| • | 099—Cocoa |

| ○ | 118—Opal |

Soie Cristale
| ✳ | 3064 |

| | 5006 (for background) |

| • | 5015 |

| ╱ | Backstitch with 2 strands of #099 |

| • | French knot with 2 strands of #099 |

Charts may be photocopied for personal use.

19

Box bottom

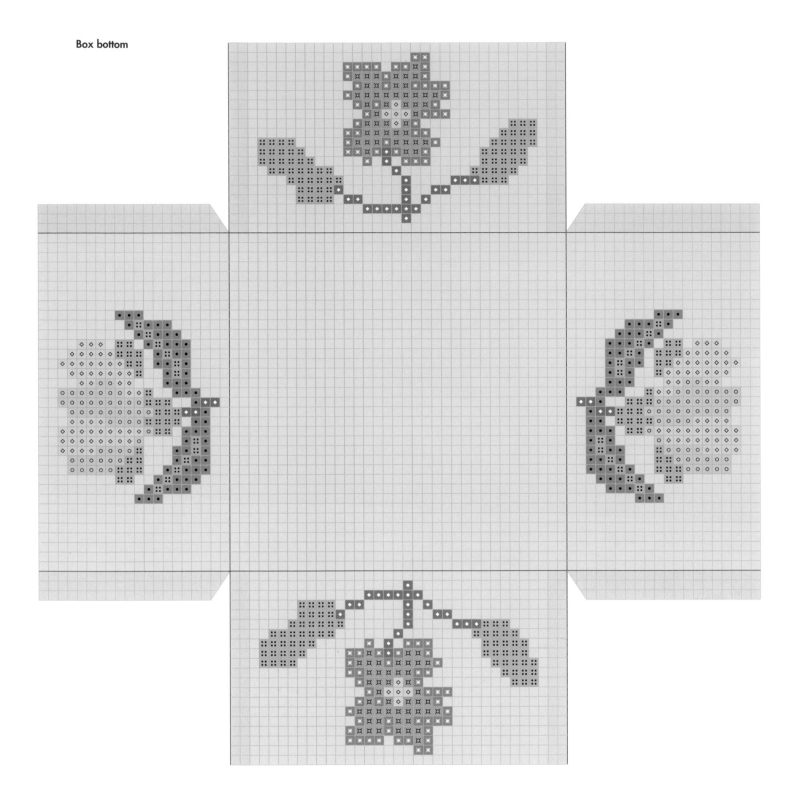

FINISHING

Cut Out Box

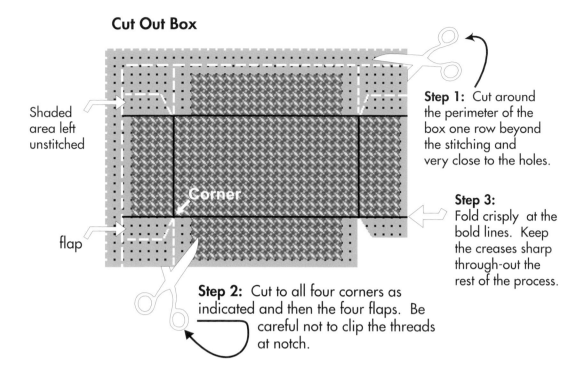

Shaded area left unstitched

flap

Step 1: Cut around the perimeter of the box one row beyond the stitching and very close to the holes.

Step 3: Fold crisply at the bold lines. Keep the creases sharp through-out the rest of the process.

Step 2: Cut to all four corners as indicated and then the four flaps. Be careful not to clip the threads at notch.

Finish Corners

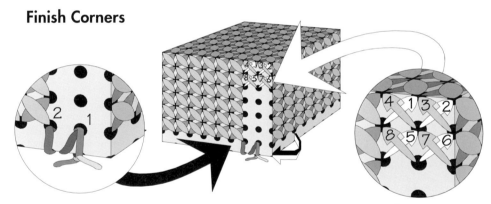

Step 1 - To Form Corners
The folded flap goes <u>under</u> the box side. To make the knot (which will hold the flap and side together), start on the inside. Stitch through hole #1, then hole #2, and then hole #1 again. Finish by tying a tight knot.

Step 2 - To Stitch Corners
Make stitch #1. Glue the end of the thread on the inside of the box. Then continue with stitch #2, #3, and so on until the side has been stitched. Glue the thread end down inside the box and then cut the knot that was holding the sides together.

Perforated paper box instructions and diagrams courtesy of Karon Killian, Whiskey Creek Ink, Marengo, Wisconsin.

Cut Out Liner

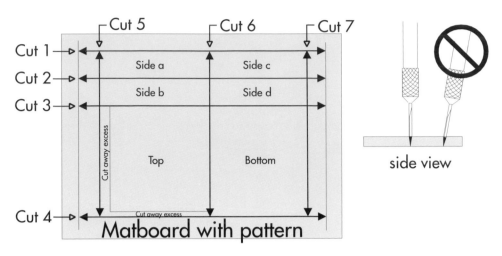

Cuts #1, 2, 3, and 4 should start and end about 1/4" from the edge of the matboard. Starting with cut #1, use a series of strokes to cut all the way through. Then continue with cuts #2, 3 and 4. Cuts #5, 6 and 7 should only be cut through partially. Once these cuts have been made, go back and cut all the way through. Then cut away the excess on the part labeled "top".

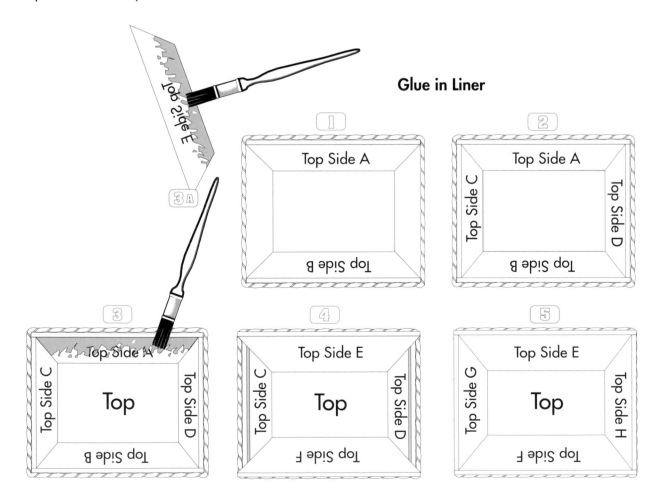

Glue in Liner

LINER PATTERNS

Actual size

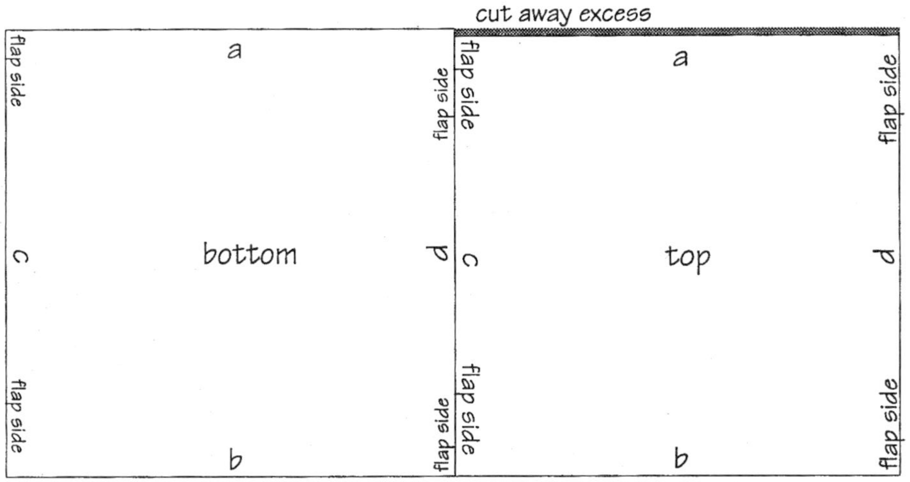

cut away excess
a
flap side
bottom
c
d
b
a
top
c
d
b
flap side
flap side
flap side
flap side
flap side
flap side
flap side
flap side

PASTE TO A SINGLE PIECE OF MATBOARD

PASTE TO A SINGLE PIECE OF MATBOARD

bottom side a
bottom side c
flap side
bottom side b
bottom side d
flap side

top side e
top side g
flap side
top side f
top side h
flap side

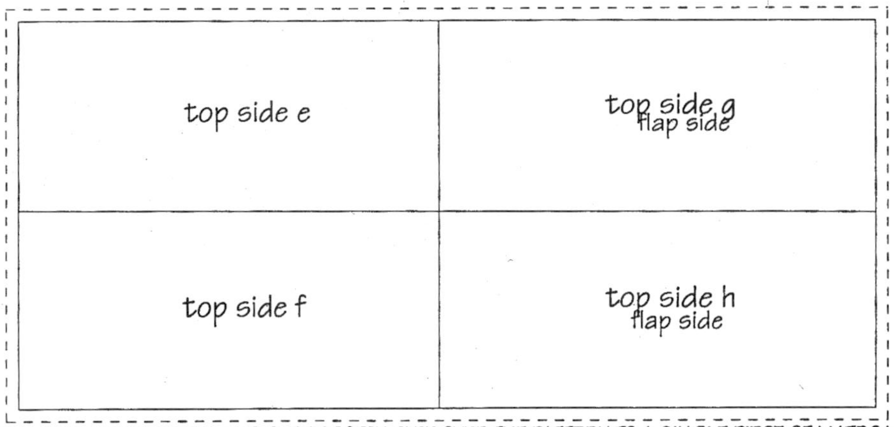

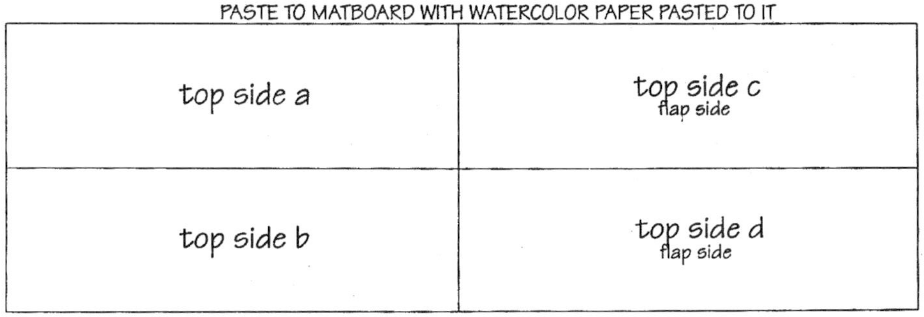

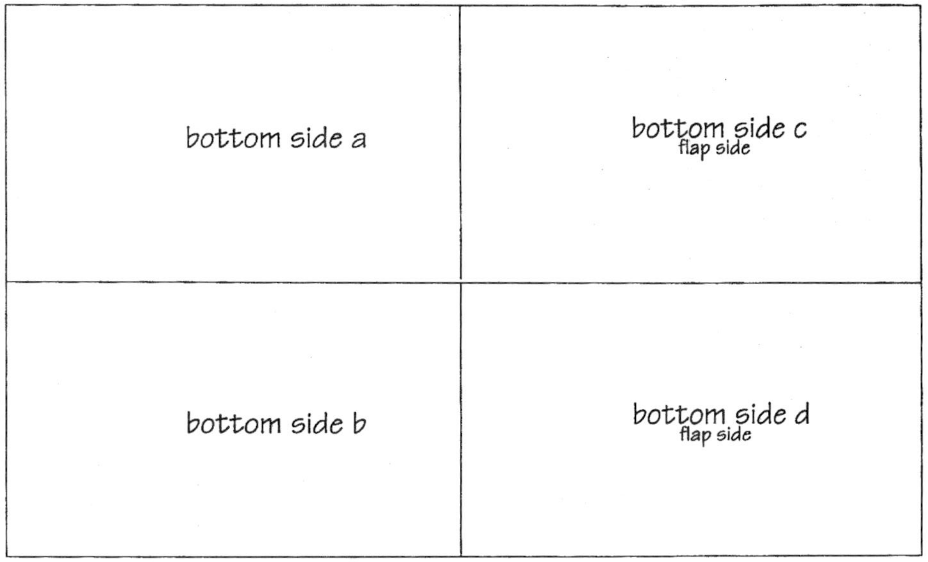

CUT ALONG DASHED LINES AND THEN SCOTCH TAPE OVER THE PATTERN TO A SINGLE PIECE OF MATBOARD

PASTE TO MATBOARD WITH WATERCOLOR PAPER PASTED TO IT

top side a
top side c
flap side
top side b
top side d
flap side

Strange Figures in a Sampler

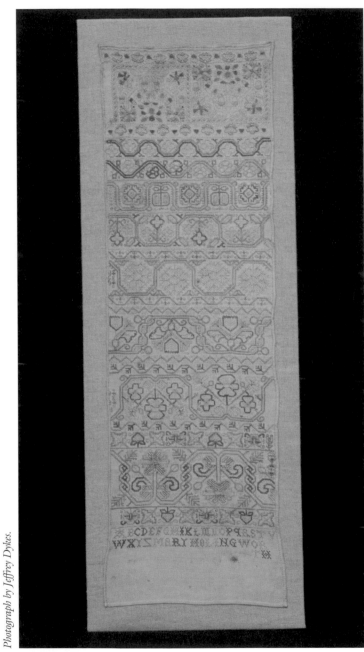

Sampler by Mary Holingworth. Silk threads on linen.

Salem or Boston, Massachusetts. Circa 1665. 25 × 7½

inches (63.5 × 19.1 cm). (4134.39).

Mary Holingworth, born in 1650 or 1652 in Salem, Massachusetts, the daughter of a successful merchant and tavern owner, stitched this band sampler while in her teens, about 1665. Embroidered with horizontal rows of floral and geometric patterns, band samplers are among the most common type of samplers to survive from seventeenth-century England and colonial America.

About ten years after completing the sampler, Mary married Philip English, an immigrant from the Isle of Jersey, who became a wealthy maritime trader. But in 1692, the couple was accused of witchcraft and imprisoned in Salem. They were able to escape to New York, returning to Salem after the witch-hunts had run their course but shortly before Mary died in 1694.

A hundred years later, in a diary entry, an acquaintance of the Englishes' great-granddaughter observed that Mary had had the best education of her time, that she wrote with ease, and that she was accomplished in the needle arts. He noted that the 2-foot-by-9-inch sampler concludes with an alphabet and her name in the usual form. But one attribute struck the writer as a foreshadower of things to come: "The figures [the floral and geometric motifs] are diversified with great ease and proportion, and there are all the stitches known to be then in use, and an endless variety of figures in right lines, after no example of nature." If not from nature, from where did these figures come?

AN ALPHABET
SAMPLER TO
CROSS-STITCH

AN ALPHABET SAMPLER TO CROSS-STITCH

O ne of the most endearing aspects of stitched samplers is the alphabet. Our alphabet, stitched on linen, is from the one stitched on the bottom of Mary Holingworth's sampler, which she made circa 1665. Floral and vine motifs divide the rows of letters on our example, which is finished as a bell pull. Individual letters may also be stitched on household textiles, including handkerchiefs, towels, and linens.

MATERIALS

Wichelt Imports 28-count Linen #86250, 100% linen fabric, Country French Cream, 1 piece 11 × 21 inches (27.9 x 53.3 cm)

DMC Embroidery Floss (Article 117), 100% cotton 6-strand thread, 8.7 yards (8 meters)/skein, 1 skein each in the colors listed in the Color Guide

Needles, tapestry size 26 (for cross-stitch) and sewing (for finishing)

Sewing thread to match linen fabric and basting

Stretcher frame

Wichelt Imports brass bell-pull hardware, #200014, 5½ inches (14.0 cm)

Finished size: 18¾ × 5½ inches (47.6 × 14.0 cm)

INSTRUCTIONS

Refer to Stitch Diagrams on pages 116–119. Whipstitch the fabric edges to prevent raveling.

Mount the fabric on the stretcher frame. Determine the center of the fabric by marking it vertically and horizontally with basting thread. Begin stitching from the center point. Using the tapestry needle and 2 strands of thread throughout, cross-stitch the design over 2 fabric threads according to the chart. Remove the fabric from the stretcher frame.

FINISHING

Sides: Count 10 fabric threads outward from each edge of the design and withdraw the eleventh thread. Fold lengthwise along the tenth thread. Allowing ½ inch (1.3 cm) for a hem on each side, trim off the excess fabric. Fold the hem allowance under twice and stitch by hand using the sewing needle and matching thread and leaving an opening at the top and bottom to accommodate the bell-pull hardware. Top and bottom: Allowing ½ inch (1.3 cm) for hems, hem to 18¾ inches (47.6 cm).

COLOR GUIDE

■ 316—Medium Antique Mauve

■ 340—Medium Blue Violet

■ 869—Very Dark Hazelnut Brown

*Each square on chart equals
2 fabric threads*

*Chart may be photocopied for
personal use.*

27

A Pastoral Picture

Photograph by Jeffrey Dykes.

Pastoral canvaswork picture by Sarah Ropes. Wool and silk threads on linen. Salem, Massachusetts. 1735–1750. 11 × 9 inches (27.9 × 22.9 cm). (133428).

Schoolgirls attending Boston-area boarding schools during the middle of the eighteenth century spent much of their time in acquiring skills in various needle arts. Embroidery was a required subject, and pastoral scenes such as this one were among the most popular themes portrayed in needlework.

Scenes were copied from or inspired by paintings, engravings, or book illustrations on many topics, including ancient Greek and Roman architecture, English country estates, landscapes, and biblical subjects. Real-life experiences were another source of inspiration. Embroidered pastoral landscapes were one of the most important types of needlework produced in colonial America; the recurring image of a female angler lent them the peculiar sobriquet of "fishing lady pictures."

Although this example, worked in tent stitch by Sarah Ropes between 1735 and 1750, lacks any fishy elements, it is full of a young woman's playfulness: note the bird, perhaps shot from the tree trunk on the left, seemingly suspended in midair above the tranquil picnicking couple, which also contrasts to the wild gestures of the girl fleeing the wolf on the right. And although the subjects are treated with naïve perspective, scale, and proportion, the refined use of color and color blending lend sophistication and show Sarah's undeniable talent with needle and thread. Sarah died in Salem in 1790 at the age of seventy-three.

A CANDLE SCREEN
TO NEEDLEPOINT
AND EMBROIDER

A CANDLE SCREEN TO
NEEDLEPOINT AND EMBROIDER

Sarah Ropes stitched her needlework picture in tent stitch and French knots using silk and wool thread on a linen ground. This candle screen, a modern adaptation of a fire screen, is worked in tent, encroaching Gobelin, and stem stitches, and French knots. It could, however, be worked entirely in tent stitch. The animal in the lower right corner has been brushed after stitching to raise its "fur."

MATERIALS

Zweigart 24-count Congress Cloth #9406, 100% cotton canvas, Pale Blue #594, 1 piece 9 × 11 inches (22.9 × 27.9 cm)

DMC Embroidery Floss (Article 117), 100% cotton 6-strand thread, 8.7 yards (8 meters)/skein, in the colors and the quantities listed in the Color Guide

DMC Medici, 100% wool nondivisible 2-strand thread, 27.3 yards (25 meters)/skein in the colors and the quantities listed in the Color Guide

Needles, tapestry size 26 (for 2 strands of embroidery floss) and size 24 (for 1 strand of embroidery floss and 1 strand of Medici wool or 2 strands of Medici wool)

Stretcher frame

Sudberry House candle screen #21001

Finished size: 7 × 5 inches (17.8 × 12.7 cm)

INSTRUCTIONS

Refer to the Stitch Diagrams on pages 116–119. Mount the fabric in the stretcher frame. Stitch the design according to the chart and the Color Key. Do not stitch the sky. Remove the canvas from the stretcher frame.

FINISHING

Brush the animal in the lower right corner with a toothbrush to fluff up the stitches. Trim off the excess fabric. Mount the finished work in the opening of the candle screen according to the manufacturer's directions.

COLOR GUIDE

DMC MEDICI

8108, 1
8207, 1
8208, 1
8306, 1
8307, 1
8369, 1
8406, 2
8407, 1
8799, 1
8800, 1

DMC EMBROIDERY FLOSS

225—Ultra Very Light Shell Pink, 1
319—Very Dark Pistachio Green, 2
320—Medium Pistachio Green, 2
334—Medium Baby Blue, 1
453—Light Shell Gray, 1
611—Drab Brown, 1
816—Garnet, 1
930—Dark Antique Blue, 1
931—Medium Antique Blue, 1
3325—Light Baby Blue, 1
3045—Dark Yellow Beige, 1
3770—Very Light Tawny, 1
3831—Dark Raspberry, 1
3832—Medium Raspberry, 1
3833—Light Raspberry, 1

Note: The numbers following the commas refer to the number of skeins needed.

1 strand #8307 & 1 strand #611—left tree trunk, stem stitch

1 strand #8406 & 1 strand #319—shadow at base of left tree trunk, stem stitch; grass foreground, encroaching Gobelin stitch

1 strand #8306 & 1 strand #611—right tree trunk, stem stitch; man's shoes & hat, tent stitch

1 strand #8407 & 1 strand #319—leaves on both trees, diamond ray stitch

1 strand #8406 & 1 strand #320—leaves on both trees, diamond ray stitch; grass midground, encroaching Gobelin stitch

1 strand #8369 & 1 strand #320—grass background, encroaching Gobelin stitch

1 strand #8108—hair, French knots (vary size of knots); animal fill, random split Gobelin

2 strands #3770—skin, tent stitch

1 strand #8799 & 1 strand #334—woman's dress outline, tent stitch

1 strand #8800 & 1 strand #3325—woman's dress fill, tent stitch

2 strands #225—woman's dress apron & bib front, tent stitch

1 strand #8207 & 1 strand #930—man's coat outline, tent stitch

1 strand #8208 & 1 strand #931—man's coat fill, tent stitch

2 strands floss #3045—basket, tent stitch; basket outline & handle, stem stitch

2 strands #611—basket, tent stitch

2 strands #816—apples, cross-stitch (over 2 threads)

1 strand #8307—animal outline, stem stitch

2 strands #3832—man's pants, tent stitch; right flower petals, directional encroaching Gobelin stitch

2 strands #3833—right flower centers, French knots

2 strands #319—right & left flower stems, stem stitch

2 strands #3831—left flower petals, stem stitch

2 strands floss #320—left flower leaves, stem stitch

2 strands #453—man's stockings, tent stitch

Chart may be photocopied for personal use.

In the Band-Sampler Tradition

Photograph by Mark Sexton.

Sampler by Sarah Erving. Silk threads on linen. Boston, Massachusetts. 1750. 16½ × 13 inches (41.9 × 33.0 cm). (M16522).

During the mid-eighteenth century, the practice of needle arts was part of the curriculum for schoolgirls throughout much of America as well as in England and continental Europe. Students were required to stitch daily, spending hours per week perfecting their skill—which seems like such a luxury today.

The sampler was a practical and common medium for recording and showing off a variety of stitches and techniques. And because much teaching occurred in a group setting, the same motifs can be found in works by many different hands. Such is the case with the figure of two men carrying a bunch of grapes between them, a motif derived from the biblical account of the exploration of Canaan on behalf of Moses and the Israelites. Stories of the Promised Land held great appeal for colonial Americans, and this popular theme can be seen repeatedly in artwork of the period.

Sarah Erving of Boston, Massachusetts, stitched the sampler shown here in 1750, when she was thirteen years old. In addition to the biblical story, she included several examples of floral and vine motifs. These geometric designs are examples of the band-sampler tradition that began in England and the American colonies in the seventeenth century and carried over well into nineteenth-century New England.

John Singleton Copley (1738–1815) painted Sarah's portrait two years after her wedding in Boston in 1762 to Samuel Waldo. The portrait is also in the museum's collection. Sarah and Samuel had six children; Sarah died in Boston in 1817.

A GUEST TOWEL TO
CROSS-STITCH

A GUEST TOWEL TO CROSS-STITCH

A variety of floral and biblical motifs grace Sarah Erving's sampler, worked in 1750 with silk thread on a linen ground. The stitched border on this guest towel incorporates the strawberries from Sarah's sampler. The towel is worked on an evenweave linen fabric with cotton embroidery floss and is finished with a four-sided edge stitch on the side hems and fringe on the ends. These materials and design are well suited for table linens as well.

MATERIALS

Zweigart 28-count Cashel #3281, 100% linen fabric, Light Sand #224, 1 piece 24 x 16 inches (61.0 × 40.6 cm)

DMC Embroidery Floss (Article 117), 100% cotton 6-strand thread, 8.7 yards (8 meters)/skein, in the colors and amounts listed in the Color Guide

Needles, tapestry size 26 (for cross-stitch) and size 24 (for pulled work)

Basting thread

Stretcher frame

Finished size: 20 × 12 inches (50.8 × 30.5 cm)

INSTRUCTIONS

Refer to Stitch Diagrams on pages 116–119. Whipstitch the fabric edges to prevent raveling. Fold the fabric in half lengthwise, then crosswise. Mark center point and baste along the vertical line. Measure 10 inches (25.4 cm) lengthwise in both directions from the horizontal center line and mark by withdrawing a horizontal thread at each end so that the fabric measures 20 inches (50.8 cm) long. Mount the fabric on the stretcher frame.

Using the size 26 needle and 2 strands of

Page 33: Pitcher and bowl courtesy of Happenstance, Fort Collins, Colorado.

embroidery floss, cross-stitch the design over 2 fabric threads, beginning 4 inches (10.2 cm) up from the withdrawn thread at the lower edge of the towel, according to the chart. Using the size 24 needle and 2 strands of #739, work the horizontal 4-sided stitch over 4 threads above the design (see illustration). Pull the stitches tightly to produce a lacy effect. Work the same 4-sided stitch below the border pattern. Repeat the strawberry border and 4-sided stitch on the other end of the fabric. Remove the fabric from the stretcher frame.

Sides: Referring to the illustration below, count 12 fabric threads outward from the 4-sided stitch in the border toward the long edge and withdraw the thirteenth vertical thread. Beginning at the top even with the horizontal 4-sided stitch border and 4 threads away, using the size 24 needle and 1 strand of #739, work Step 1 (the first half) of the vertical 4-sided stitch. After working Step 1, fold the edge of the fabric under at the edge of the row of vertical stitches, crease, and work Step 2. Work the other side of the towel in the same way.

FINISHING

Cut the fabric very close to the stitches in the space left by the withdrawn thirteenth thread on each side. To make the fringe: Count down 12 threads from the lower edge of the 4-sided-stitch pattern and remove all the horizontal threads below the twelfth thread to the first withdrawn thread. Trim off the excess fabric below the fringe.

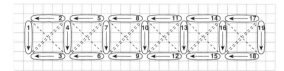

VERTICAL 4-SIDED STITCH

Step 1: Follow the green markings (first half of the stitch), using 1 strand of #739.
Fold the fabric along the black line.
Step 2: Follow the blue markings (second half of the stitch), using 1 strand of #739.
The red dotted line indicates the withdrawn thirteenth thread.

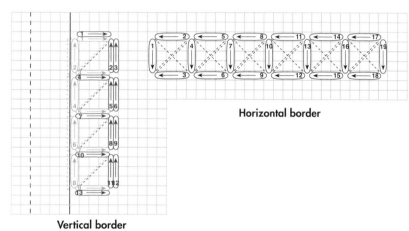

Horizontal border

Vertical border

COLOR GUIDE AND SYMBOL KEY

- 956—Geranium, 1
- 957—Pale Geranium, 1
- 963—Ultra Very Light Dusty Rose, 2
- 991—Dark Aquamarine, 1
- 3811—Very Light Turquoise, 1
- :: 3816— Celadon Green, 1
- + 963 and 3816 (use 1 strand of each)
- 739—Ultra Very Light Tan, 1 (4-sided stitch)

Note: The numbers following the color names refer to the number of skeins needed.

Chart may be photocopied for personal use.

Each square on the chart equals 2 fabric threads

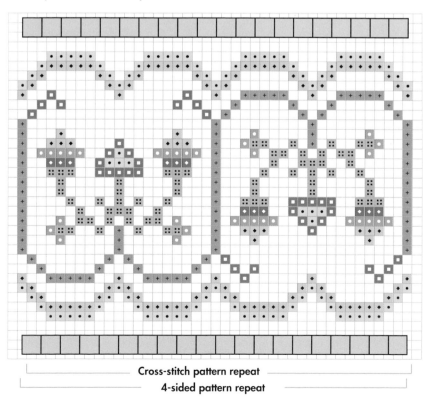

Cross-stitch pattern repeat
4-sided pattern repeat

A Paradise on Canvas

Pastoral canvaswork picture by Sarah Chamberlain. Wool, silk, and metallic threads on linen.

Boston or Salem, Massachusetts. Circa 1765. 8⅜ × 10 inches (21.3 × 25.4 cm). (128281).

Much of the pastoral canvaswork attributed to eighteenth-century New England depicted an idealized vision of the natural world, a kind of paradise on Earth. Gardens and landscapes were always neat and tidy, and the human figures who populated them were similarly manicured. The blue-petticoated yellow dress and high-heeled shoes of the woman in this picture would seem to be more appropriate to a parlor than to an orchard. The decorative stomacher stitched in metallic threads is an extravagant touch. The woman is in the process of plucking fruit from the tree, perhaps a symbol of fertility. A dog accompanies her on her outing and birds, including a rather large blue one, fly overhead.

Whether Sarah Chamberlain herself ever appeared alfresco in such finery or whether she could have afforded such luxury is not known. The Massachusetts needlewoman stitched the picture circa 1765, when she would have been about fifteen years old, and it's wonderful to imagine a young woman fancying herself in just this situation. Sarah died on April 27, 1796.

A WALL MIRROR
INSERT TO
NEEDLEPOINT
AND EMBROIDER

A WALL MIRROR INSERT TO NEEDLEPOINT AND EMBROIDER

The idyllic setting from Sarah Chamberlain's needlework picture is adapted here for an insert in a wall mirror. The young woman, dressed in the fashion of the eighteenth century, picks apples from a tree as her dog waits by her side. Sarah worked her picture in tent stitch with silk and wool thread on linen; ours uses a combination of tent stitch and embroidery stitches and is worked with silk threads on a cotton ground.

MATERIALS

Zweigart 24-count Congress Cloth #9406, 100% cotton fabric, Pale Blue #594, 1 piece 9 × 11 inches (22.9 × 27.9 cm)

Kreinik Silk Mori, 100% silk 6-ply thread, 5 meters (5.5 yards)/skein, in the quantities and colors listed in the Color Guide

Needle, tapestry size 24

Stretcher frame

Sudberry House narrow gold mirror, #2209G

Finished size of design: 7 × 5 inches (17.8 × 12.7 cm)

INSTRUCTIONS

Refer to Stitch Diagrams on pages 116 -119. Mount the canvas in the stretcher frame. Using the tapestry needle and 2 strands of silk unless otherwise instructed, stitch the design according to the chart and the following. Do not stitch the sky.

Apples (on the tree on the right): Use padded satin stitch and #1116 with vertical stitches on top.

Apple tree foliage: Use tent stitch and 1 strand each of #4204 and #4206.

Apple tree trunk: Use stem stitch and #7134.

Woman's figure: Use tent stitch and #5014 to outline the underskirt; fill with tent stitch and #5093. Use tent stitch and 1 strand each of #7124 and #9032 for the flesh. Use tent stitch and #7126 for the sleeves and the jacket body. Use double cross stitch and 1 strand each of #7126 and #9034 for the overskirt. Use alternating oblong cross stitch and #9034 for the bib and cuffs. Use tent stitch and #9034 for the hair.

Left tree trunks: Use stem stitch and #7136 for the dark areas and #7134 for the light areas.

Leaves on left trees: Use detached chain stitch and #4204, #4206, #4063, or 1 strand each of #4204 and #4206, randomly.

Bird: Use stem stitch and #5014 to outline; use long-and-short stitch and #5053 and #5093, randomly, for fill.

Flowers: Use satin stitch, following colors on the chart.

Flower leaves: Use long-and-short stitch and 1 strand each of #4204 and #4206, randomly.

Dog: Use stem stitch and 1 strand of #7134 to outline; use split Gobelin stitch and #7024 to fill the dark areas and #7126 to fill the light areas.

Grasses: Use encroaching Gobelin stitch from background to foreground and follow the chart for color changes. In the background start by using 2 strands of #4204 and gradually switch to using 1 strand each of #4204 and #4206. For the mid-ground, start with 2 strands of #4206 and then 1 strand each of #4206 and #4063. In the foreground, use 2 strands of #4063.

Flower stem: Use stem stitch and #7134.

Remove the canvas from the stretcher frame.

FINISHING

Trim off the excess fabric. Mount the finished work in the opening in the wall mirror according to the manufacturer's directions.

Page 37: Pitcher courtesy of Sense of Place, Fort Collins, Colorado.

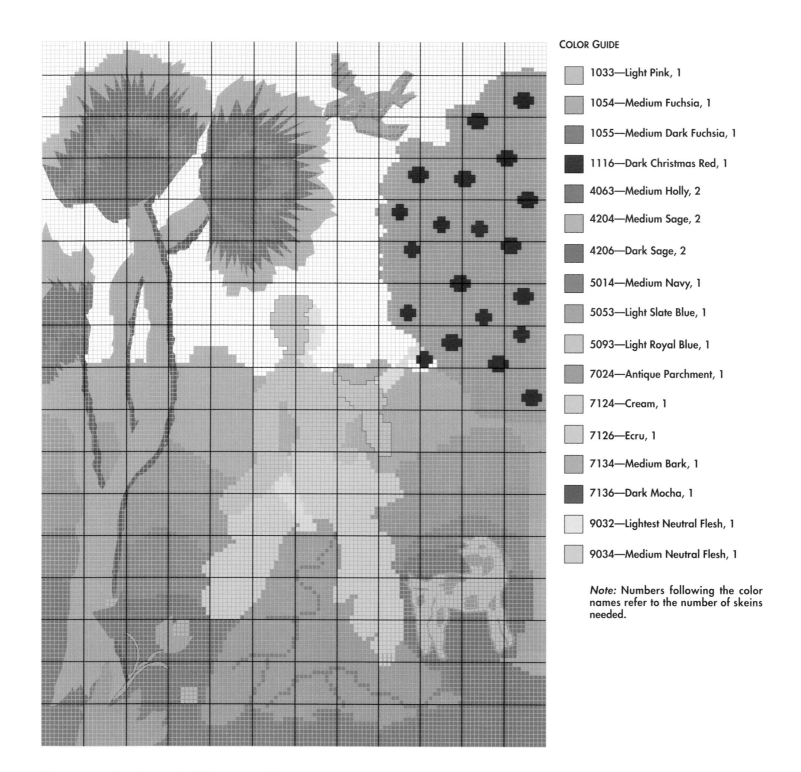

COLOR GUIDE

- 1033—Light Pink, 1
- 1054—Medium Fuchsia, 1
- 1055—Medium Dark Fuchsia, 1
- 1116—Dark Christmas Red, 1
- 4063—Medium Holly, 2
- 4204—Medium Sage, 2
- 4206—Dark Sage, 2
- 5014—Medium Navy, 1
- 5053—Light Slate Blue, 1
- 5093—Light Royal Blue, 1
- 7024—Antique Parchment, 1
- 7124—Cream, 1
- 7126—Ecru, 1
- 7134—Medium Bark, 1
- 7136—Dark Mocha, 1
- 9032—Lightest Neutral Flesh, 1
- 9034—Medium Neutral Flesh, 1

Note: Numbers following the color names refer to the number of skeins needed.

Chart may be photocopied for personal use.

A Waistcoat for a Fashion Plate

*I*magine dressing in a lavishly embroidered waistcoat, a jacket of lush brocade, knee breeches, silk stockings, and buckled shoes, and then going out for an evening

Waistcoat front. Silk threads on satin. Probably France. Late eighteenth century. 24½ inches (62.2 cm) long. (128074).

at the cockfights. The feminine flamboyance that allowed lace on men's clothing and the masculine grit that tolerated fight-until-death public brutality may seem outrageous according to twenty-first century sensibilities, but they were the custom among many gentlemen of the eighteenth century.

As jackets evolved to reveal more and more of the waistcoat, the latter became increasingly ornamental. It could be made to match or contrast with the suit, both in color and material, and it offered a unique opportunity for the expression of individual style and taste. The waistcoat was constructed of rich fabric and embellished with embroidery, metallic braid, trim, and fancy buttons. The late-eighteenth-century example shown here was probably embroidered in France, and it is embellished with floral embroidery along the front opening, a characteristic common to many other waistcoats of the period. Less common is the appearance of landscapes or figures, especially a scene as graphic as the cockfight featured at the bottom of the vest. Pocket flaps were given special attention, and the waistcoat was given the finishing touch with just the right buttons. The waistcoat's donor asserted that it was owned by the Lawrence family and was worn to a reception for George Washington (1732–1799).

AN EYEGLASS
CASE TO
EMBROIDER

AN EYEGLASS CASE TO EMBROIDER

The elaborately embroidered satin waistcoat was worked in satin stitch. Satin and stem stitches in silk thread are used in this satin eyeglass case to replicate the floral motif found on the waistcoat's pocket flaps. We added a twisted cord edging made from the silk thread; but the case is just as lovely without the edging.

MATERIALS

Satin fabric, Ivory, 2 pieces, 12 × 18 inches (30.5 × 45.7 cm) each

Caron Collection Waterlilies, 100% hand-dyed silk, 12-strand thread, 6 yards (5.5 meters)/skein, 1 skein each in the colors listed in the Color Guide

Caron Collection Soie Cristale, 100% silk 12-strand thread, 6 yards (5.5 meters)/skein, 1 skein each in the colors listed in the Color Guide

Needles, chenille size 26 (for embroidery) and sewing (for finishing)

Sewing thread to match fabric (for finishing) and a contrasting color (for basting)

Embroidery hoop, 8-inch (20.3-cm)

Batting, lightweight, ¼ yard (0.2 meter)

Pencil, HB

Tissue paper

Finished size: 6¾ × 3¼ inches (17.1 × 8.3 cm), excluding twisted cord

INSTRUCTIONS

Refer to Stitch Diagrams on pages 116–119. Trace the pattern onto the tissue paper. Center the traced design on one piece of the fabric; pin. Center the fabric in the hoop. Using the sewing needle and contrasting thread, baste the tissue onto the fabric with small stitches, following the traced lines. Tear off the tissue. Check the fabric to ensure that the entire design has been stitched.

Using the chenille needle and 1 strand and stem stitch for all stems and 2 strands and satin stitch for the flowers and leaves, work the design according to the color numbers on the pattern. Remove the fabric from the hoop.

FINISHING

Remove any of the basting stitches. Weave the thread ends into the back of the work. From the second piece of fabric, cut a rectangle 8 × 7¾ inches (20.3 × 19.7 cm) for the lining. From the batting, cut a rectangle 6¾ × 6½ inches (17.1 × 16.5 cm). Trim the stitched fabric to a rectangle 7¾ × 7½ inches (19.7 × 19.1 cm). Fold the stitched fabric right sides together and using the sewing needle and matching thread, sew the side and bottom seams, leaving the top seam open. Trim the seams. Tack the batting to the remaining seam allowances. Turn the case right side out. Fold the lining fabric wrong sides together and sew the side and bottom seams, leaving the top seam open. Trim the seams and clip the corners. Turn the lining wrong side out. Insert the lining into the case matching the seam of the lining and case. Fold ½ inch (1.3 cm) of the raw edge of the case to the inside; fold ⅝ inch (1.6 cm) of the raw edge of the lining inward toward the batting and whipstitch the edges. Steam press under a pressing cloth. Attach a twisted cord, if desired.

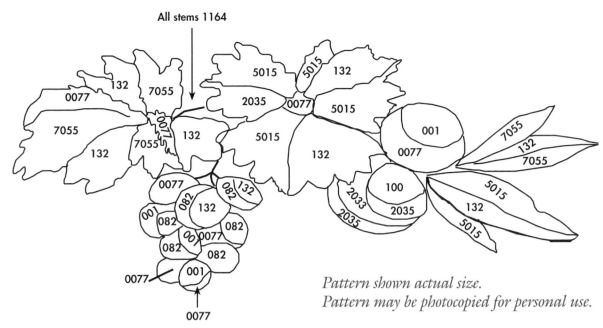

All stems 1164

Pattern shown actual size.
Pattern may be photocopied for personal use.

COLOR GUIDE

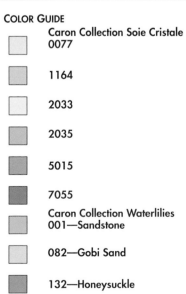

Caron Collection Soie Cristale
0077

1164

2033

2035

5015

7055

Caron Collection Waterlilies
001—Sandstone

082—Gobi Sand

132—Honeysuckle

A PAIR OF
COVERED
BUTTONS TO
EMBROIDER

A PAIR OF COVERED BUTTONS TO EMBROIDER

A leaf from the pocket flap of the late-eighteenth-century silk-on-satin waistcoat (on page 40) here embellishes a pair of buttons covered in ivory satin and sewn onto a small pillow. Worked with silk thread in satin stitch and mounted on purchased button backs, the buttons are easy to make.

MATERIALS

Satin fabric, Ivory, for two buttons, 1 piece 8 × 11 inches (20.3 × 27.9 cm)

Caron Collection Soie Cristale, 100% silk 12-strand thread, 6 yards (5.5 meters)/skein, 1 skein each in the colors listed in the Color Guide

Needles, crewel size 10 (for embroidery) and sewing (for basting)

Sewing thread (for basting)

Embroidery hoop, 4-inch (10.2-cm)

Dritz Cover Button Kit

Tissue paper

Finished size of each button: 1¼ inches (3.2 cm) in diameter

INSTRUCTIONS

Refer to Stitch Diagrams on page 116–119. Cut the fabric into two pieces; reserve one half for the second button. Trace the pattern (omitting the outer circle) onto the tissue paper. Center the tissue pattern on the fabric; pin. Center the fabric in the hoop. Using the sewing needle, baste the tissue onto the fabric with small stitches, following the traced lines. Tear off the tissue. Check the fabric to ensure that the entire design has been stitched. Using the crewel needle and 2 strands of thread throughout, work stem stitch for the stem, straight stitch for the tips of the green leaf, and satin stitch for the remaining areas. The colors are indicated on the illustration. Remove the fabric from the hoop. Work the second button in the same way.

FINISHING

Remove any basting stitches. Weave the thread ends into the back of the work. Cut the fabric in a circle 2½ inches (6.4 cm) in diameter. Assemble the buttons according to the directions on the button kit.

COLOR GUIDE

- 1164
- 5015
- 7053
- 7055

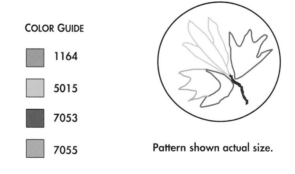

Pattern shown actual size.

Pattern may be photocopied for personal use.

1164 for tips

5015

7053

7055

7053

1164

Elaborate Embroidery and an Unusual Motif

Sampler by Mary Richardson. Silk threads on linen. Salem, Massachusetts. 1783. 24¼ × 23½ inches (61.6 × 59.7 cm). (123559).

In the days before pattern books became available, the sampler was a sort of notebook for recording a needlewoman's repertoire of embroidery stitches. By the seventeenth century, a sampler had evolved into a school exercise that was usually signed and dated by the maker. Eventually, the sampler came to be viewed as a work of art executed for its own sake.

The sampler shown here was stitched by Mary Richardson of Salem, Massachusetts, and was completed in 1783. Mary, born in 1772, married Penn Townsend (1772–1846), a mariner, in 1793; they had four children. She died in 1824.

The elaborately embroidered border combines elements of the English pastoral landscape tradition—a lady and gentleman in stylish clothing flanked by birds and trees—with the symmetry and regularity of New England samplers—lateral floral vines that encircle the sampler. An unusual feature is the winged angel head at the top center of the border, a motif more commonly seen carved into a gravestone.

The long surface stitch worked in crinkled silk floss is characteristic of samplers made at schools in Salem and the surrounding region during the last quarter of the eighteenth century.

A PICTURE FRAME TO EMBROIDER

A padded frame of stylized flowers, inspired by the floral vine with oversized roses and carnations on Mary Richardson's 1783 sampler, holds a photograph. This one uses satin, stem, and long-and-short stitches and French knots on 22-count cotton fabric, but you could alternatively work the frame with a variety of needlepoint stitches and wool yarn on 18-count canvas.

MATERIALS

Zweigart 22-count Janina #3318, 100% cotton fabric, Williamsburg Green, 1 piece 13 × 15 inches (33.0 × 38.1 cm)

Needle Necessities Floss Overdyed, 100% cotton 6-strand thread, 20 yards (18.3 meters)/skein, 1 skein each in the colors listed in the Color Guide

Needle Necessities Pearl 8 Overdyed, 100% cotton nondivisible thread, 20 yards (18.3 meters)/skein, 1 skein in the color listed in the Color Guide

DMC Embroidery Floss (Article 117), 100% cotton 6-strand thread, 8.7 yards (8 meters)/skein, 1 skein in the color listed in the Color Guide

Needles, crewel size 5 (for embroidery) and sewing (for basting)

Sewing thread (for basting)

Stretcher frame

Finished size: 8 × 10 inches (20.3 × 25.4 cm); opening, 6⅝ × 4⅝ inches (16.8 × 11.7 cm)

INSTRUCTIONS

Refer to Stitch Diagrams on pages 116–119. Whipstitch the fabric edges to prevent raveling.

Baste the design on the fabric. Mount the fabric on the stretcher frame. Using the crewel needle and 3 strands of thread throughout except for the large vine (use 1 strand), stitch the design according to the pattern and the following.

Large vine: Use stem stitch and 1 strand of Needle Necessities Pearl 8 Overdyed #8133.

Stems: Use stem stitch and Needle Necessities Pearl 8 Overdyed #8133.

Small branches and leaf veins: Use stem stitch and Needle Necessities Floss Overdyed #133.

Large flowers: Use long-and-short stitch and the colors indicated on the pattern.

Calyxes and leaves: Use satin stitch and Needle Necessities Floss Overdyed #1331.

Buds and five-petaled flowers: Use satin stitch and the colors indicated on the pattern.

All flower centers: Use French knots and 3 strands of DMC #729.

Remove the fabric from the stretcher frame.

FINISHING

Take the stitched piece to a needlework finisher or frame shop for padding and mounting on a frame.

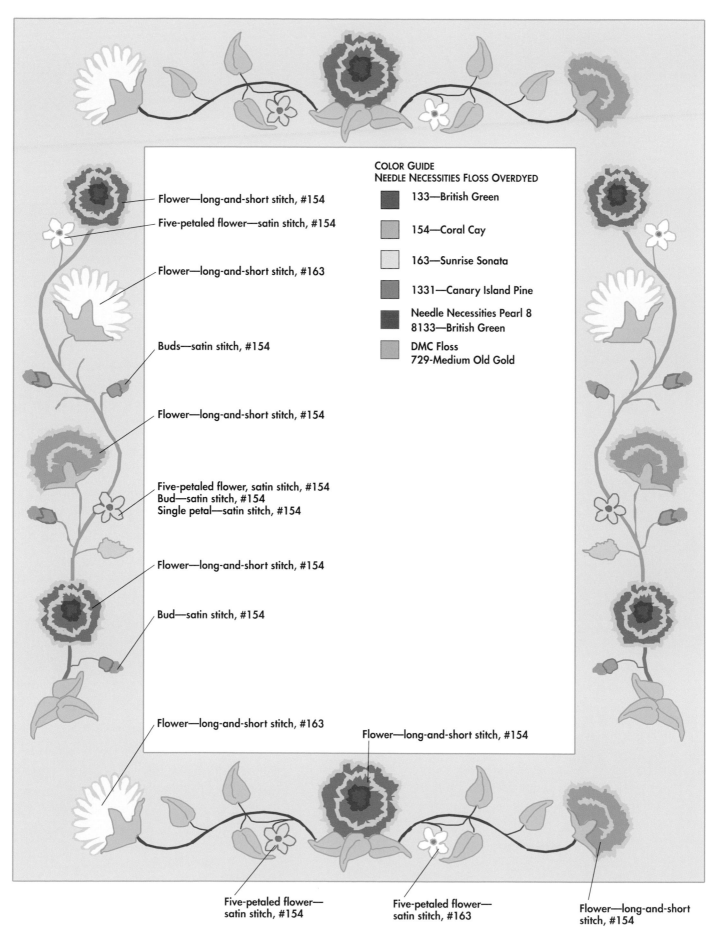

COLOR GUIDE
NEEDLE NECESSITIES FLOSS OVERDYED

133—British Green

154—Coral Cay

163—Sunrise Sonata

1331—Canary Island Pine

Needle Necessities Pearl 8
8133—British Green

DMC Floss
729-Medium Old Gold

Flower—long-and-short stitch, #154

Five-petaled flower—satin stitch, #154

Flower—long-and-short stitch, #163

Buds—satin stitch, #154

Flower—long-and-short stitch, #154

Five-petaled flower, satin stitch, #154
Bud—satin stitch, #154
Single petal—satin stitch, #154

Flower—long-and-short stitch, #154

Bud—satin stitch, #154

Flower—long-and-short stitch, #163

Flower—long-and-short stitch, #154

Five-petaled flower—
satin stitch, #154

Five-petaled flower—
satin stitch, #163

Flower—long-and-short
stitch, #154

Pattern shown is reduced 10% of actual size.
Pattern may be photocopied for personal use.

Note: The right side is a mirror image
of the left side.

Pastoral and Neoclassical

Sampler by Sally Martin Bowen. Silk threads on linen. Marblehead, Massachusetts. Circa 1800. 20⅛ × 16¼ inches (51.1 × 41.3 cm). (135370).

The stitching of samplers by young women in America during the seventeenth century and through the early twentieth century provided an opportunity for the maker to show her agility with several stitches and techniques on a single cloth. Over time, regional distinctions among samplers evolved, reflecting the differing tastes and talents of teachers in different schools.

The sampler stitched by Sally Martin Bowen, who was born in 1789, is a fine example of the distinctive style that developed during the late eighteenth century in Marblehead, Massachusetts, a coastal community on Boston's North Shore. This one was probably completed about 1800, but for some reason the date once stitched as part of the inscription at the center of the sampler was removed sometime after its completion. The verse, shown near the center on the sampler, is from a hymn by the English theologian Isaac Watts (1678–1748). Sally Bowen died in 1872.

Green linen provides a vibrant background for the sampler's rural landscape elements. The grass in the lower border is stitched with vertical rows of pale blue cross-stitch interspersed with long stalks in stem stitch. The urns with flowers reflect the neoclassical style that dominated art and decorative arts in early-nineteenth-century America.

A JOURNAL COVER TO EMBROIDER

Sally Bowen chose pastel silk thread on green linen for her sampler. We selected the basket of flowers in the lower left corner as the centerpiece for this journal or book cover. A black slubbed silk fabric is the ground for silk- and metallic-thread work; it is appliquéd to a raw linen cover.

MATERIALS

Slubbed silk fabric, Black, 1 piece 6 x 6 inches (15.2 × 15.2 cm)

Kreinik Silk Mori, 100% silk 6-strand thread, 5 meters (5.5 yards)/skein, 1 skein each in the colors listed in the Color Guide

Kreinik Cord, single ply metallic thread, 50 meters (55 yards)/reel, 002C Gold, 1 reel

Kreinik Very Fine (#4) Braid, metallic braid, 11 meters (12 yards)/reel, 205C Antique Gold, 1 reel

Needles, crewel size 10 (for stitching and couching) and size 8 (for laid threads), and sewing (for basting and finishing)

Sewing threads in matching color (for finishing) and contrasting color (for basting)

Embroidery hoop, 4-inch (10.2-cm)

Tissue paper

Fabric-covered journal

Finished size: 2¾ × 3⅜ inches (7.0 × 8.6 cm)

INSTRUCTIONS

Refer to Stitch Diagrams on pages 116–119. Trace the pattern onto the tissue paper. Center the tissue pattern on the fabric; pin. Center the fabric in the hoop. Using the sewing needle and basting thread, baste the tissue onto the fabric with small stitches, following the traced lines.

Tear off the tissue. Check the fabric to ensure that the entire design has been stitched.

Using the size 10 needle and 1 strand of Silk Mori, work the flowers as indicated on the illustration. For the basket top, lay four separate 2-strand sets of 7086 Silk Mori with the size 8 needle; couch each set with 002C and the size 10 needle as it is laid. For the basket bottom, lay three 2-strand sets of 7086 Silk Mori and couch each as it is laid. Fill in the space between the top and bottom of the basket by laying strands of 205C with the size 8 needle; couch with 002C and the size 10 needle. Outline the entire design with 002C, using a fine, closely spaced stem stitch to create a cloisonné look. Remove the fabric from the hoop.

FINISHING

Remove any of the basting stitches. Weave the thread ends into the back of the work. Allowing ½ inch (1.3 cm) for a hem on all four sides, trim off the excess fabric. Fold the hem allowance under twice and stitch by hand using the sewing needle and black thread. Mount the cover on the book to determine placement of the silk fabric. Pin the fabric to the center of the front of the cover, remove the cover, and stitch the silk fabric to it by hand using the sewing needle and the black thread.

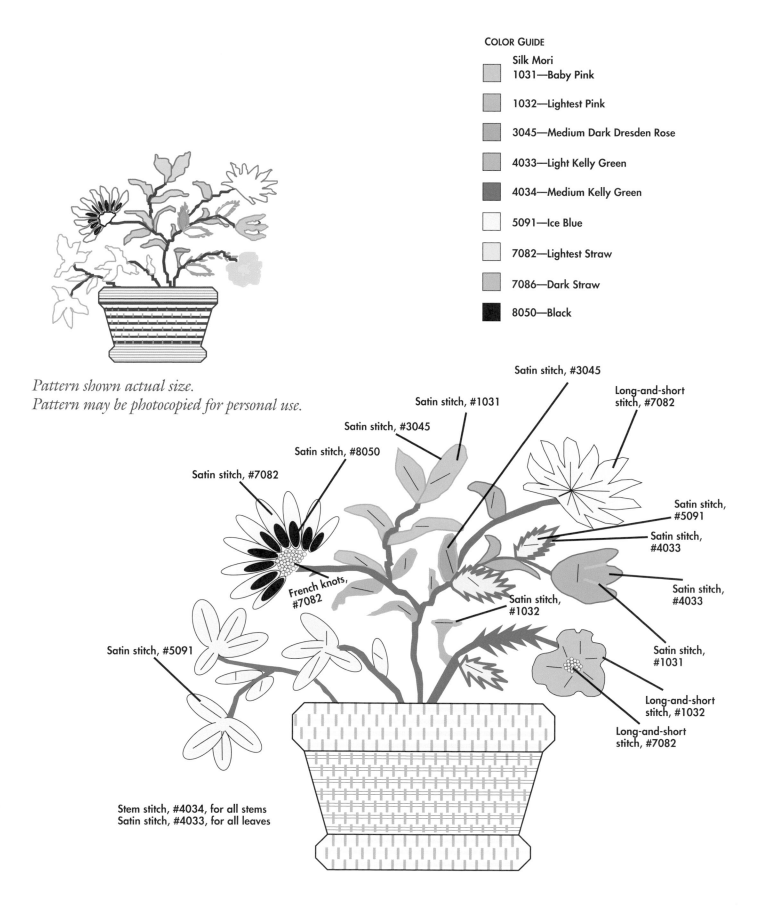

COLOR GUIDE

Silk Mori

1031—Baby Pink

1032—Lightest Pink

3045—Medium Dark Dresden Rose

4033—Light Kelly Green

4034—Medium Kelly Green

5091—Ice Blue

7082—Lightest Straw

7086—Dark Straw

8050—Black

Pattern shown actual size.
Pattern may be photocopied for personal use.

Satin stitch, #3045

Satin stitch, #1031

Long-and-short stitch, #7082

Satin stitch, #3045

Satin stitch, #8050

Satin stitch, #7082

Satin stitch, #5091

Satin stitch, #4033

Satin stitch, #4033

French knots, #7082

Satin stitch, #1032

Satin stitch, #1031

Satin stitch, #5091

Long-and-short stitch, #1032

Long-and-short stitch, #7082

Stem stitch, #4034, for all stems
Satin stitch, #4033, for all leaves

Alphabets, Flowers, and Virtues

Needlework techniques and design elements, like customs and traditions, have a way of traveling to new regions, and often they are adopted or adapted by the residents of these new areas. It is often impossible to know the origin of a given example or style. That is the case with this sampler stitched by Sarah Todd in 1807. Although it has been attributed to Salem, Massachusetts, certain attributes, including the incorporation of birds and baskets of flowers as motifs, suggest that it might have originated in the Merrimack River Valley region in northern Massachusetts or in southern New Hampshire. Only the name and birth date of the maker and the year of completion are known with certainty; this information is stitched into the center of the work.

The ability to render the alphabet in different scripts and styles was an important skill for an eighteenth- or nineteenth-century American woman to acquire. Letters and numbers were used not only to sign pieces and to mark household linens but to form the inscriptions that were the centerpieces of many samplers. The verse on this sampler expresses a prevalent belief that industriousness was an antidote to sin and inappropriate behavior.

Photograph by Jeffrey Dykes.

Sampler by Sarah Todd. Silk threads on linen. Northeastern Massachusetts or New Hampshire. 1807. 26 × 25 ½ inches (66.0 × 64.8 cm). (133922).

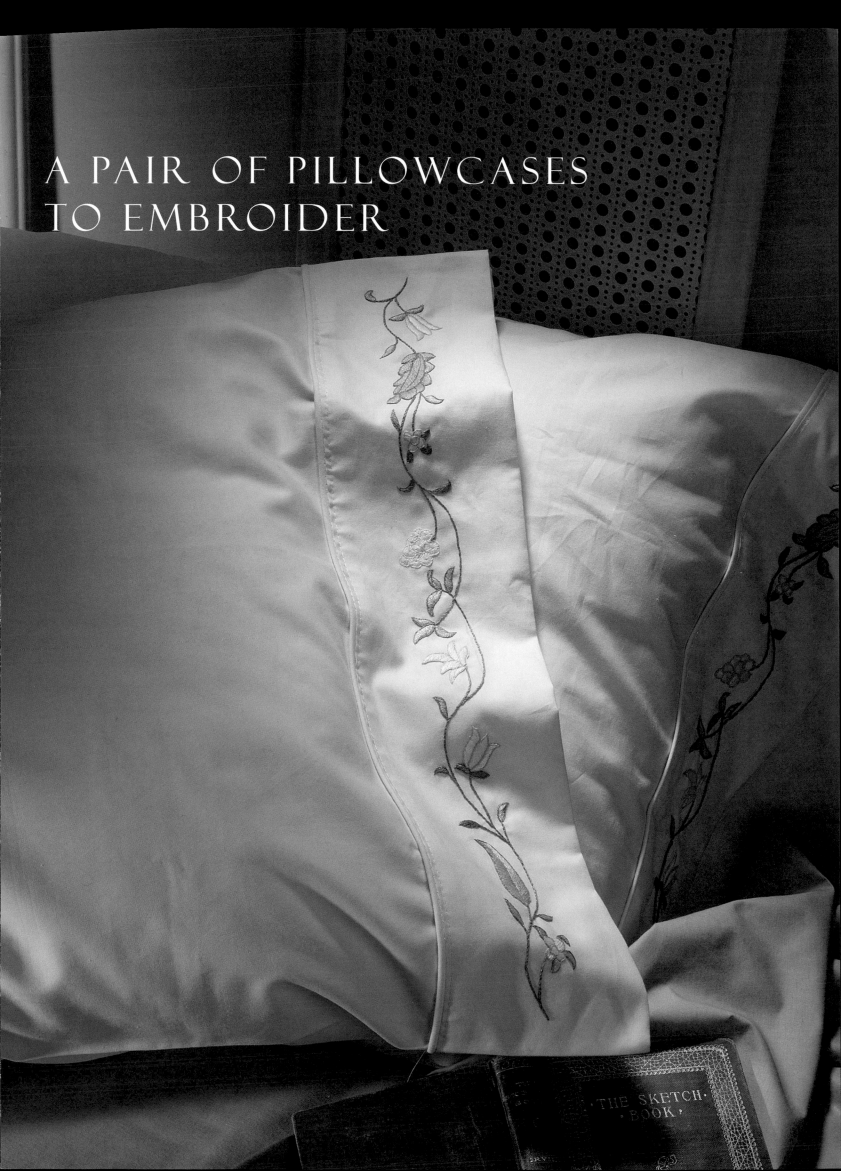

A PAIR OF PILLOWCASES TO EMBROIDER

A PAIR OF PILLOWCASES TO EMBROIDER

A meandering floral vine, taken from the lower border of Sarah Todd's sampler, is here worked on the borders of crisp, white Egyptian cotton pillowcases using stem, satin, straight, and circular buttonhole stitches. The motif would be just as attractive as a border for guest towels or table napkins.

MATERIALS

Pillowcases, 100% Egyptian cotton, White, one pair

DMC Embroidery Floss (Article 117), 100% cotton 6-strand thread, 8.7 yards (8 meters)/skein, 1 skein each in the colors listed in the Color Guide

Needles, crewel size 8 (for embroidery) and sewing (for finishing)

Sewing thread, contrasting color (for basting) and white (for finishing)

Embroidery hoop, 4-inch (10.2-cm)

Tissue paper

Finished size of design: 18⅛ inches (46.0 cm) long

INSTRUCTIONS

Refer to Stitch Diagrams on pages 116–119. Remove the machine stitching from the hem of each pillowcase. Press open the fold at the edge of the case; you will be stitching through only the outer layer of fabric. Trace the pattern, matching the center points, onto the tissue paper. Pin the tissue pattern to the fabric. Using the sewing needle and darker thread, baste the tissue onto the fabric with small stitches, following the traced lines. Tear off the tissue. Check the fabric to ensure that the entire design has been stitched. Mount the single thickness of pillowcase hem in the hoop.

Using the crewel needle, work as indicated below, following the directional lines on the pattern for all of the fill stitches.

Stems: Use stem stitch and 2 strands of #562.

Leaves: Use stem stitch and 1 strand of #562 for outlines and satin stitch and 2 strands of #562 or #3817 (dark or light green) for fills.

Flowers except for buttonhole flowers: Use stem stitch and 1 strand of #3821 for all outlines and satin stitch and 2 strands of #3078 for fills.

Buttonhole flowers: Use buttonhole stitch worked in the round and 1 strand of #3078.

Remove the pillowcase from the hoop. Work the second pillowcase in the same way.

FINISHING

Remove any of the basting stitches. Weave the thread ends into the back of the work. Fold, press, and restitch the hem in place by hand using the sewing needle and white thread. Finish the second pillowcase in the same way.

COLOR GUIDE

562—Medium Jade

3078—Very Light Golden Yellow

3817—Light Celadon Green

3821—Straw

Pattern shown actual size.
Pattern may be photocopied for personal use.

Center point

Right side

Left side

Center point

57

A Stag and a Leopard

Photograph by Sotheby's.

Windsor stools with needlework upholstery. Maker unknown. Wool threads on linen. New England.

1810–1830. Each stool: 15 inches (38.1 cm) tall; each seat: 10 × 13 inches (25.4 × 33.0 cm).

(137665.2AB).

Windsor chairs are character-ized by their spindle back, turned, splayed legs, and, usually, a saddle seat. Though clearly influenced by its English forebears, this style of furniture is probably the most popular to emerge from eigh-teenth-century America. Windsor furniture in-cluded various styles of chairs and stools.

These Windsor stools, with bamboo-turned legs and a painted finish, are unusual because they are taller than the more common squat footstools; they would have functioned as footrests or seats.

The original petit-point seat covers shown here, worked between 1810 and 1830, feature a re-clining stag or leopard surrounded by a floral wreath. The embroidery is done with wool thread on a linen ground. Exotic and familiar animal motifs such as these can also be found on hooked rugs, stoneware crocks, and wall murals made during the early nineteenth century. It is possi-ble that the motifs were derived from a woodcut or other popular illustration. The upholstery also includes the original green wool fringe attached with a row of brass tacks.

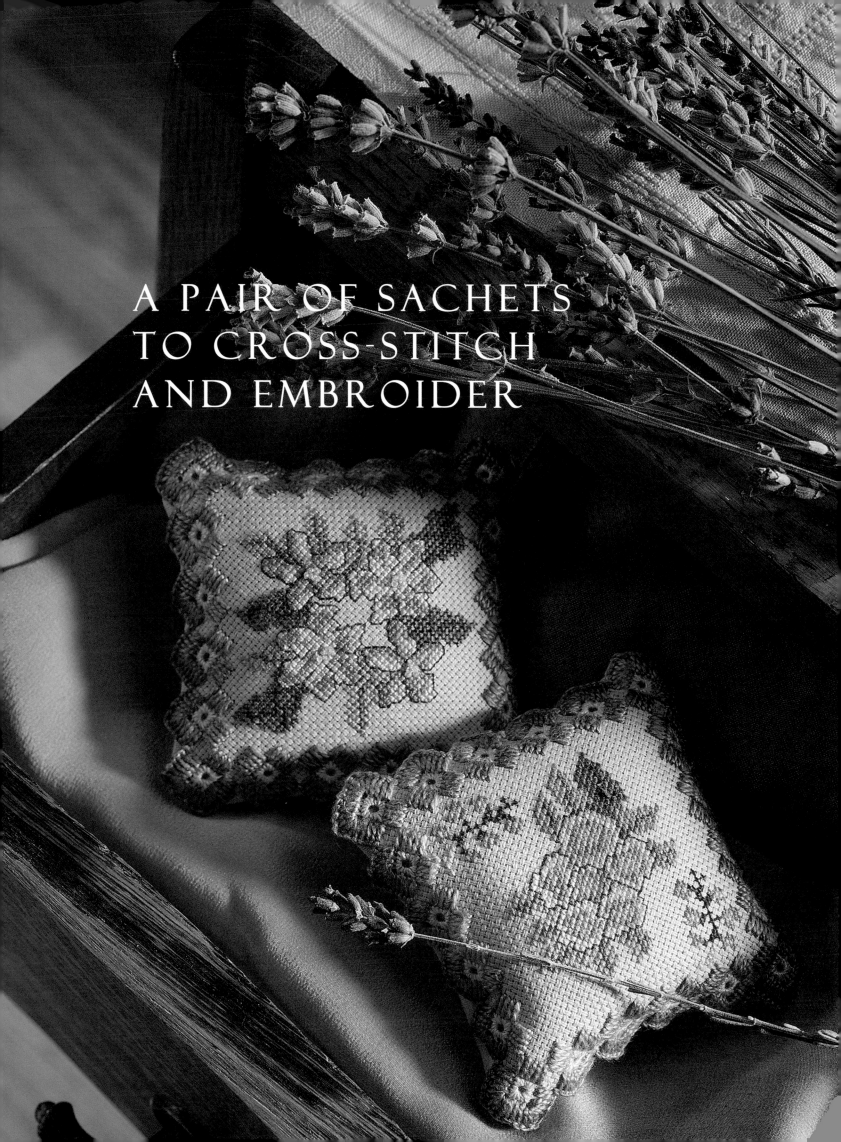

A PAIR OF SACHETS
TO CROSS-STITCH
AND EMBROIDER

A PAIR OF SACHETS TO
CROSS-STITCH AND EMBROIDER

Aflower from each of the floral wreaths on the two Windsor stools is the focus for these two small sachets worked on a cotton evenweave fabric. The stitched kloster blocks with eyelets in the center form a ready-made edging. Fill the sachets with lavender, as we did, to scent dresser drawers or closets, or with emery or sand to make pincushions.

MATERIALS

Zweigart 22-count Hardanger #1008, 100% cotton fabric, Antique Mushroom #308, 2 pieces 6 x 6 inches (15.2 × 15.2 cm) each

DMC Embroidery Floss (Article 117), 100% cotton 6-strand thread, 8.7 yards (8 meters)/skein, 1 skein each in the colors listed in the Color Guide

Caron Collection Watercolours, 100% hand-dyed cotton 3-strand thread, 10 yards (9 meters)/skein, 1 skein in the color listed in the Color Guide

Caron Collection Wildflowers, 100% solid and hand-dyed cotton nondivisible thread, 36 yards (33 meters)/skein, 1 skein in the color listed in the Color Guide

Kreinik Blending Filament, 50 meters (55 yards)/reel, 1 reel in the color listed in the Color Guide

Needles, tapestry size 26 (for embroidery) and sewing (for finishing)

Sewing thread to match cotton fabric (for finishing) and a contrasting color (for basting)

Muslin, ⅛ yard, natural

Potpourri or emery for filler

Finished size of each sachet: 3½ × 3½ inches (8.9 × 8.9 cm)

INSTRUCTIONS

Refer to Stitch Diagrams on pages 116–119. Whipstitch the fabric to prevent raveling.

Determine the center of one fabric square by marking it vertically and horizontally with basting thread.

Begin stitching at the center point. Using the tapestry needle and 1 strand of thread, cross-stitch the floral design according to the diagram.

Use 1 strand of Watercolours #121 Evergreen for the kloster blocks and Wildflowers #116 Cotton Candy for the eyelets (see illustration). Follow the diagram, which shows that the outer portions of the kloster blocks are worked in buttonhole stitch and the inner portions are straight stitch. Place a few French knots made with 2 strands of the Blending Filament in the centers of the flowers. Using 1 strand of DMC floss, backstitch the flowers with the colors indicated on the chart. Work the second piece of fabric in the same way.

FINISHING

Cut each finished sachet top close to the kloster blocks. Cut two 3½-inch (8.9-cm) squares of muslin for each sachet. Place the muslin squares together, pin, and stitch 3 sides by hand using the sewing needle and the matching thread and leaving a ¼-inch (6-mm) seam allowance. Fill the muslin with potpourri or emery. Fold in the remaining seam allowance and sew the muslin pillow closed. Stitch the sachet top to the muslin pillow so that the points formed by the kloster blocks extend beyond the pillow edges. Finish the second sachet in the same way.

DMC Floss
500—Very Dark Blue Green

501—Dark Blue Green

813—Light Blue

826—Medium Blue

962—Medium Dusty Rose

963—Ultra Very Light Dusty Rose

3350—Ultra Dark Dusty Rose (for backstitch)

3750—Very Dark Antique Blue (for backstitch)

3753—Ultra Very Light Antique Blue

3816—Celadon Green

Caron Collection Watercolours
121—Evergreen (for kloster blocks)

Caron Collection Wildflowers
116—Cotton Candy (for eyelets)

Kreinik Blending Filament
091—Yellow

Eyelet. Begin at 1 and work straight stitch into the center of a kloster block. Continue around the square, working from the edge to the center.

Diagrams may be photocopied for personal use.

Note: Read the interior floral design as a cross-stitch chart; read the surrounding kloster block and eyelet stitches as a stitch diagram.

61

The Dance

The Dance, painted and embroidered picture by Frances Leverett. Watercolor and silk chenille threads on silk. Boston or the North Shore of Massachusetts. Circa 1815. 17 × 23 inches (43.2 × 58.4 cm). (129212).

Who would suspect that these happy dancers are about to become prey to the actions of an unscrupulous landlord? But that's the story behind this scene so meticulously embroidered by Frances Leverett, the daughter of William (1770–1811) and Charlotte Leverett (1795–?) of Roxbury, Massachusetts. The subject is derived from the poem "The Deserted Village" by Oliver Goldsmith (1730?–1774), whose works were popular among young women in eighteenth-century America. Frances likely saw an engraving or book illustration of the scene and interpreted it in needlework. She completed it about 1815, two years before her marriage to John Shays of Danvers, Massachusetts.

This picture is executed in watercolor and silk chenille threads. (Chenille thread, which derives its name from the French word for "caterpillar," has a hairy or fuzzy appearance.) The raised chenille threads and the careful use of color and shading create an overall effect of softness and subtle light. The faces, hands and arms, and the sky have been painted in, perhaps by a professional artist or, just as likely, by Frances herself.

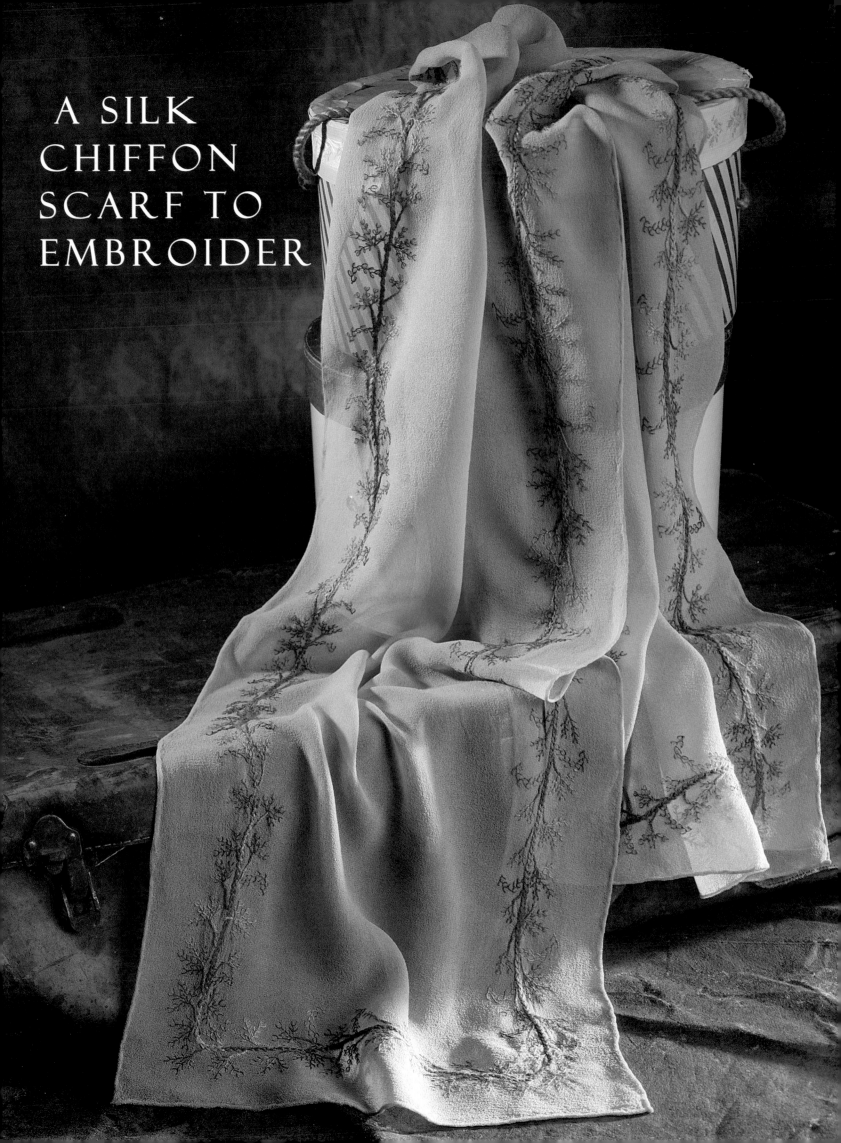

A SILK
CHIFFON
SCARF TO
EMBROIDER

A SILK CHIFFON SCARF TO EMBROIDER

The garland of flowers emanating from the basket in the lower left of Frances Leverett's painted and embroidered picture inspired the flowing, free-form design in twisted chain, feather, and fly stitches bordering this silk chiffon scarf, which measures 72 inches (182.9 cm) long. Maintaining consistent tension while stitching to combat the stretchiness of the chiffon will reward the stitcher with a lovely and versatile accessory. (Our scarf was hand dyed before stitching.)

MATERIALS

Silk chiffon scarf, 72 × 14 inches (182.9 × 35.6 cm)

Caron Collection Waterlilies, 100% hand-painted silk 12-strand thread, 6 yards (5.5 meters)/skein, 1 skein each in the colors listed in the Color Guide

Needle, crewel size 12

Fabric pencil

Finished width of design: 2 inches (5.1 cm)

INSTRUCTIONS

Refer to Stitch Diagrams on pages 116–119. Use the crewel needle throughout. Using the fabric pencil, mark the center stem line onto the fabric ¾ inch (1.9 cm) in from the rolled hem all the way around the edge. Work the center stem first so that subsequent stitching will be anchored to it. Beginning and ending all threads in the back of the twisted chain stitch, work the center stem in twisted chain stitch using 3 strands of #061. Work the supporting branches in stem stitch with 1 strand alternating #061, #106, and #139. Work the fan shapes at the end of the branches in fly stitch with 1 strand alternating #106 and #137. Work the remaining foliage in feather stitch with 1 strand of #139.

FINISHING

Weave the thread ends into the back of the twisted chain stitch.

Page 63: Silk chiffon scarf hand dyed by Elda Kohls, Fort Collins, Colorado. Leather suitcase and hatboxes courtesy of Happenstance, Fort Collins, Colorado.

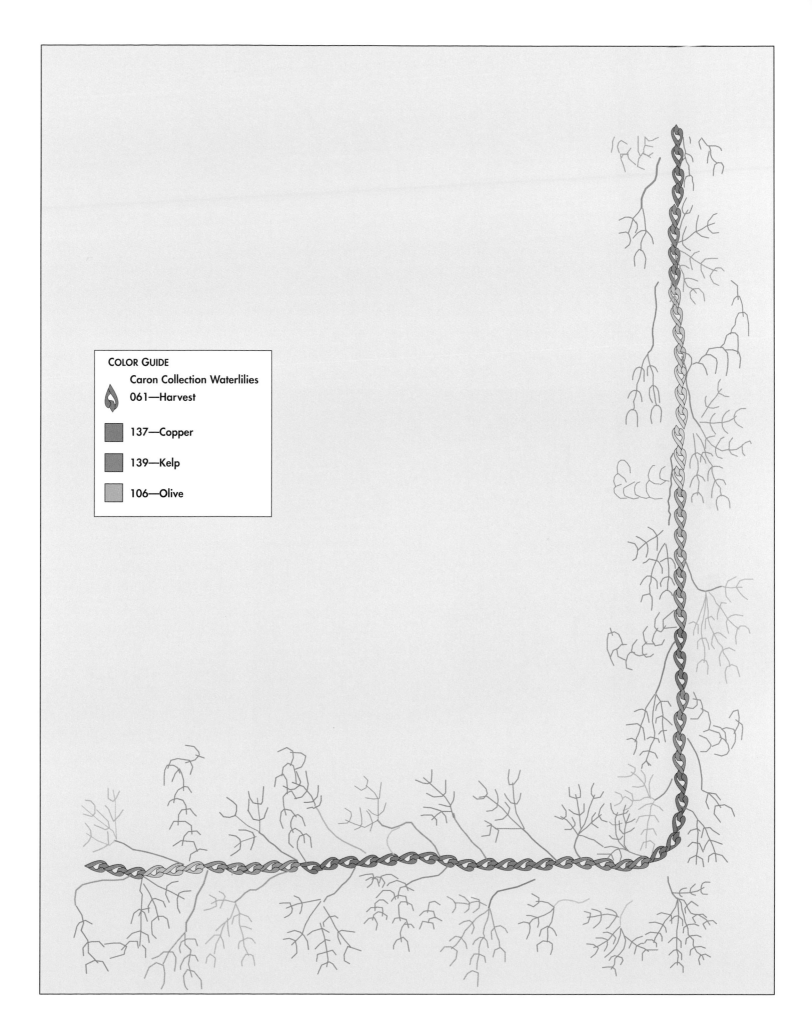

COLOR GUIDE

Caron Collection Waterlilies

061—Harvest

137—Copper

139—Kelp

106—Olive

A Stylish Collar

The collar has been through many modifications in its long history as a fashion accessory. Egyptian pharaohs wore heavy ones of gold and lapis lazuli. Sixteenth-century Europe saw stiff, starched ruffs that were ruched and often edged with embroidery and lace. During the seventeenth century, New England Puritans adopted a plain, uncomfortable collar that epitomized the morals and ethics of their society, while colonists in the South opted for the somewhat more frivolous cavalier look. They have been made of silk, linen, wool, even celluloid.

Collars such as the one shown here were worn over the wide necklines of women's dresses that were fashionable in the early part of the nineteenth century. Using embroidery floss and perhaps a bit of lace or fringe to dress up plain fabric, a woman of almost any means could create a unique collar for any occasion.

This collar, worn in New England about 1825, is made of soft white wool lined with white silk and is adorned with a vine of grapes and leaves worked in chenille floss. The silk chenille on the flat wool ground looks like velvet. A wool fringe edges the collar, and ribbon ties fasten it in place.

Photograph by Jeffrey Dykes.

Collar. Maker unknown. Silk chenille threads on wool; wool fringe.

New England. 1825–1835. 23¾ × 15¼ inches (60.3 × 38.7 cm). (127197).

A RECIPE
BOX TOP TO
EMBROIDER

A RECIPE BOX TOP TO EMBROIDER

The unknown maker of the collar used chenille floss to stitch the vine, leaves, and clusters of grapes on the white wool fabric. The vines, one leaf, and a cluster of grapes are here stitched in silk threads on a cotton ground to make a fabric insert for the top of a wooden recipe box. Tightly packed French knots form three-dimensional grapes; stem and long-and-short stitches are used to create the leaf and vines.

MATERIALS

Zweigart 24-count Congressa #3990, 100% cotton fabric, White #100, 1 piece 7 × 9 inches (17.8 × 22.9 cm)

Gumnut Yarns, 100% hand-dyed silk non-divisible thread, 27.3 yards (25 meters)/skein, 1 skein each in the colors listed in the Color Guide

Needle, tapestry size 24

Basting thread

Stretcher frame

Sudberry House Recipe Box #99081, wood finish

Finished size of the insert: 4½ × 6½ inches (11.4 × 16.5 cm)

INSTRUCTIONS

Refer to Stitch Diagrams on pages 116–119. Whipstitch the fabric edges to prevent raveling. Trace the pattern onto the tissue paper. Pin the tissue pattern to the fabric, centering the traced design on the fabric. Using the sewing needle and basting thread, baste the tissue onto the fabric with small stitches, following the traced lines. Tear off the tissue.

Check the fabric to ensure that the entire design has been stitched. Mount the fabric on the stretcher frame.

Use 1 strand of thread throughout. Work a double row of stem stitches for the branches with #B629. Work one row of stem stitches for the curly vines according to the pattern. Work the leaf in long-and-short stitch.

Work each grape in densely packed French knots using J-Sapphire Dark and #B237 in random order. Use occasional touches of the lighter purple, #B273, in some of the grapes for highlights. Wrap the needle once for the French knots on the perimeter of the grapes; wrap it twice for the inner knots to make them stand taller. Leave a little space between the grapes for definition. Work a few areas of stem stitches with #B629 to indicate stems running through the cluster of grapes.

FINISHING

Weave the thread ends into the back of the work. Trim off the excess fabric. Mount the finished work in the opening in the box top according to the manufacturer's directions.

B629

B629

B629

B569

B629

J-Emerald

J-Emerald

J-Emerald

B569

J-Emerald

B569

Pattern shown actual size.
Pattern may be photocopied for personal use.

The Language of Flowers

Christmas dinner in a well-to-do nineteenth-century American home may have included such exotic foods as sweetbread pâté, quail with truffles, and Nesselrode pudding, but it is unlikely that the woman of the house wore a garment quite as fine as this one while preparing the comestibles. In fact, the intricate embroidery and lace edging on this purple silk apron elevate it to a work of art.

The exquisite floral motifs are worked in chenille embroidery, ribbon work, and crepe work. The ribbon-work flowers are made by folding and embroidering silk ribbon in shaded colors while folding and stitching strips of sheer silk crepe forms blossoms in low relief.

The borders and waistband of this apron, which was stitched between 1830 and 1840, contain more than a dozen recognizable varieties of flowers, whose multicolored blossoms are associated with the once-popular "language of flowers." According to this convention, each kind of flower represents a different "meaning" or sentiment, usually with romantic implications. For example, the moss rose was code for "pleasure without alloy." Thus, besides the obvious visual statement rendered by the embroidery, a proclamation of love or secret message from the stitcher is most likely inherent in the work.

Photograph by Jeffrey Dykes.

Apron with floral embroidery. Maker unknown. Silk chenille threads, silk ribbon, and silk crepe on silk. United States. 1830–1840.

31 × 31¼ inches (78.7 × 79.4 cm). (134970).

A CHATELAINE
TO EMBROIDER

A CHATELAINE TO EMBROIDER

Needleworkers have used chatelaines for centuries to keep their tools organized and accessible. This chatelaine is adorned with an adaptation of the floral motif found on the borders and waist of the silk apron. Grosgrain ribbons, sewn onto each end, hold needlework tools. Needle weaving, spider-web, detached chain, and straight stitches, and French knots, all worked with silk thread, offer variety and hours of stitching entertainment.

MATERIALS

Zweigart 32-count Lugana #3835, 50% cotton/40% rayon fabric, Blue Spruce #3984/578, 1 piece 50 × 5 inches (127 × 12.7 cm)

JL Walsh Silk Perle, 100% 8-strand silk thread, 12 yards (11 meters)/skein, 1 skein each in the colors listed in the Color Guide

Needles, tapestry size 24 (for embroidery) and sewing (for finishing)

Sewing thread to match fabric

Grosgrain ribbon to match fabric, 2 yards (1.8 meters), ⅜-inch (1.0-cm) wide

Embroidery hoop, 5-inch

Finished size: 45 × 2 inches (114.3 × 5.1 cm)

INSTRUCTIONS

Refer to Stitch Diagrams on pages 116–119. Whipstitch the fabric edges to prevent raveling. Measure 2½ inches (6.4 cm) in from each end of the fabric and mark for the hem. Fold the fabric in half lengthwise and crosswise to find the center point and baste along the folds. Mount the fabric in the embroidery hoop, if desired. Repeat the charted motif three times at each end of the fabric above the hem marker. The placement of the elements is indicated on the diagram. The main stem connects the repeats, and should lie beneath any overlapping elements.

Using the tapestry needle and 3 strands of Silk Perle #32, work the main stem in stem stitch. Use 1 strand of Silk Perle #32 combined with 1 strand of Silk Perle #31 to work the other stems in stem stitch. Use a random selection of 2 strands of the greens to work all of the leaves in random ray stitch. Stitch the flowers according to the diagram, using 1 strand of Silk Perle except for those worked in the spider-web stitch, which requires 2 strands.

FINISHING

Fold the fabric strip lengthwise, right sides together, pin, and stitch a ½-inch (1.3-cm) seam along all the raw edges, leaving a 3-inch (7.6-cm) opening in the middle of the long side. Trim the seams. Turn the chatelaine right side out, turn in the remaining raw edges, and sew the opening closed. Cut the ribbon into six 12-inch (30.5-cm) lengths; sew three lengths onto each end of the chatelaine, equally spaced across the ends.

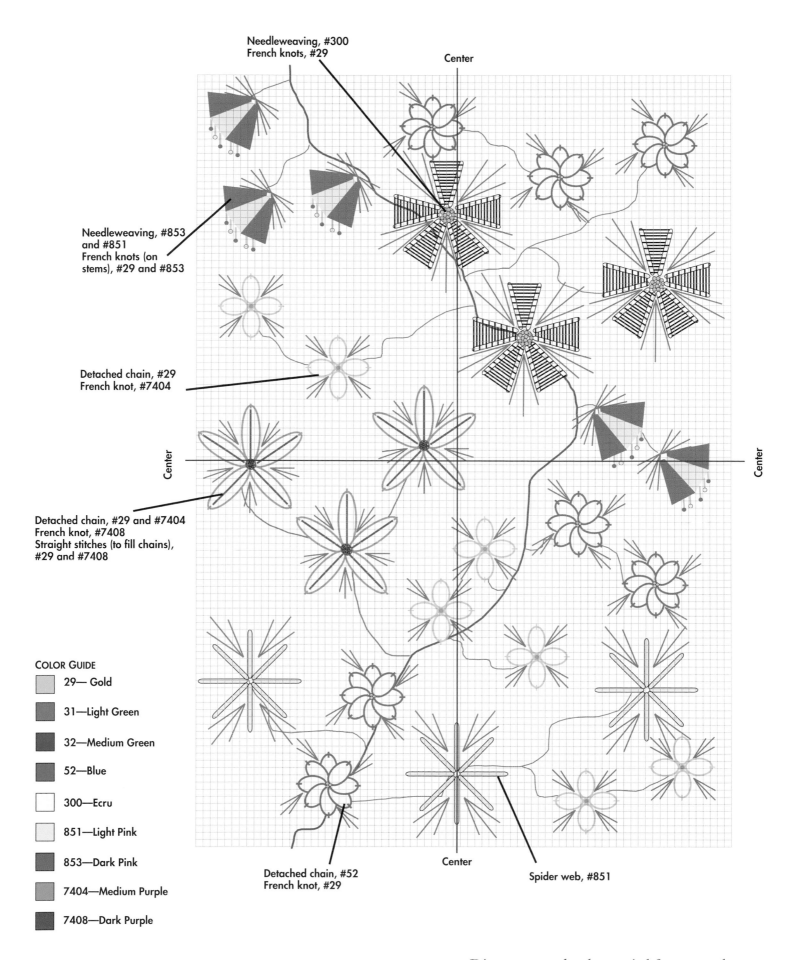

Needleweaving, #300
French knots, #29

Center

Needleweaving, #853
and #851
French knots (on
stems), #29 and #853

Detached chain, #29
French knot, #7404

Center

Detached chain, #29 and #7404
French knot, #7408
Straight stitches (to fill chains),
#29 and #7408

Center

COLOR GUIDE

29— Gold

31—Light Green

32—Medium Green

52—Blue

300—Ecru

851—Light Pink

853—Dark Pink

7404—Medium Purple

7408—Dark Purple

Detached chain, #52
French knot, #29

Center

Spider web, #851

Diagram may be photocopied for personal use.

73

Mary Berry True's Table Cover

Cover by Mary Berry True; table by Joseph True. Wool threads on linen. Salem, Massachusetts. 1840. Cover: 28½ inches (72.4 cm) in diameter. (133540 and 133541, respectively).

Today, many of us would consider a hand-carved mahogany table a luxury, one that we might put in a corner of a room, out of harm's way, and adorn with a decorative as well as protective cover. A custom-made needlepoint cover for that same table would be wildly extravagant. But for Joseph and Mary Berry True, who married in 1809, this combination was part of the everyday furnishings in their mid-nineteenth-century home in Salem, Massachusetts. The table was designed for multiple uses. It could be a parlor center table, a tea table, or used for reading, and when it was put in the corner of a room, its top could be tilted up to save space.

Joseph True was a woodcarver and cabinetmaker by trade, and he most likely built this table for his family's personal use. Typical of many objects that filled New England homes during this period, both table and cover are influenced by a variety of stylistic sources. The table reflects the transition from the neoclassical to Victorian styles. The same styles are seen in Mary's table cover: the center medallion is a typical neoclassical element, but the floral bouquet that comprises it is evidence of the romantic Victorian-era love of nature and the picturesque. The cover's flower-and-leaf edging includes Mary's initials and the year of completion: 1840, fourteen years before her death; Joseph died in 1873.

A CANDLE RING TO CROSS-STITCH

A CANDLE RING TO CROSS-STITCH

Surround a pillar candle with a colorful stitched candle ring. The flowers and leaves are from the edge of Mary Berry True's table covering, which she worked in needlepoint with wool threads on a linen ground. The candle ring is worked on a linen stitchband with prefinished edges.

MATERIALS

Zweigart 14-count Stitchband #7339, 100% linen fabric, Driftwood #013, 1 piece the circumference of the candle plus 1½ inches (3.8 cm)

Caron Collection Wildflowers, 100% solid and hand-dyed cotton nondivisible thread, 36 yards (33 meters)/skein, 1 skein each in the colors listed in the Color Guide

Needles, tapestry size 24 (for cross-stitch) and sewing (for finishing)

Sewing thread to match the stitchband

Velcro or snap fasteners for finishing

Pillar candle

Finished size of design: 9 × 3¼ inches (22.9 x 8.3 cm)

INSTRUCTIONS

Refer to Stitch Diagrams on pages 116–119. Using the tapestry needle and 1 strand of thread throughout, cross-stitch the design according to the chart.

FINISHING

Place the finished piece around the pillar candle, overlapping the ends by 1 inch (2.5 cm). Fold under twice and pin a ½-inch (1.3-cm) hem on each raw edge. Hem by hand using a sewing needle and matching thread. Sew on three Velcro or snap fasteners.

Photo page 75: Candle stand courtesy of Sense of Place, Fort Collins, Colorado. Candles courtesy of The Cupboard, Fort Collins, Colorado.

Center →

← Center

COLOR GUIDE

–	047—Camouflage	
×	117—Fresh Pink	
✳	140—Blackwatch	
○	141—Alpine Moss	
◇	146—Moonglow	
•	148—Rosebud	
■	149—Cherry Cordial	
⦂⦂	159—Silver Blue	
+	169—Moss	
◆	7001—Williamsburg Blue	

Chart may be photocopied for personal use.

Master Appleton's Christening Dress

Photographs by Jeffrey Dykes.

Christening dress. Maker unknown. Cotton threads on cotton. Boston, Massachusetts. 1847. 41 inches (104.1 cm) long. (117556).

Women throughout history have made use of the needle arts to create articles, both utilitarian and decorative, that reflect their love and devotion to family, but the anticipated birth of a child offers a singular opportunity for them to express their maternal love and family identity. The practice of dressing infants in elaborate robes for a christening ceremony became common in eighteenth-century America. And because white has long been considered the color of purity, it is fitting that intricate whitework embroidery was used to embellish this garment worn by Francis Henry Appleton at his christening at St. Paul's Church in Boston on November 1, 1847. Francis, who died in Boston in 1939, grew up to serve in the Massachusetts Senate in 1902 and 1903.

Excellent workmanship in whitework is imperative because there is no color to distract the eye from the path of the thread. The technique reached a peak of popularity in the nineteenth century, when it appeared on handkerchiefs, caps, collars, sleeves, and cuffs, even on undergarments that were intended to impress only a woman's most intimate companion.

Although a large-scale industry developed in England, Scotland, and Ireland to produce work such as that shown here, which is known as Ayrshire whitework, amateur embroiderers used printed patterns to create their own versions of the floral stitchery.

A CHRISTENING
CLOTH TO
EMBROIDER

A CHRISTENING CLOTH TO EMBROIDER

The elegant whitework floral motifs from Francis Henry Appleton's christening dress are worked with silk thread on this Swiss batiste christening cloth. It would be equally suitable as a bride's handkerchief. Experienced embroiderers will find this a satisfying project.

MATERIALS

Capitol Imports Swiss Batiste, 100% cotton fabric, White #B241, 1 piece 14 inches (35.6 cm) square

Rainbow Gallery Subtlety Silk Pearl, 100% silk nondivisible thread, 30 yards (27.4 meters)/card, White #Y802, 1 card

Rainbow Gallery Splendor, 100% silk 12-strand thread, 8 yards (7.3 meters)/card, White #S802, 1 card

Needles, tapestry size 26 (for Subtlety) and crewel size 10 (for Splendor)

Embroidery hoop, 5 inch (12.7 cm)

Pencil, HB

Spray starch

Finished size: 9¾ inches (24.8 cm) square

INSTRUCTIONS

Refer to Stitch Diagrams on pages 116–119. Try to make the beginnings and endings of your threads as invisible as possible. Use a tiny knot on the back of your work to begin a thread. To end a thread, make a sewing knot on the back of the work, then work the tail into the back of the stitches, and trim it close to your work.

Measure 1¾ inches (4.4 cm) in from one side of the fabric and withdraw one thread. If it breaks as you are pulling it out, carefully pick up the same thread with a pin and con-tinue to withdraw it. Turn the fabric a quarter turn and repeat the previous step. Measure 10½ inches (26.7 cm) across the fabric from the thread that you withdrew and withdraw another thread. Turn the fabric a quarter turn and repeat the previous step. You will have a square marked by the pulled threads that measures 10½ inches (26.7 cm) square.

Spray the fabric with 3 or 4 coats of starch, letting the fabric dry in between coats. Press the fabric smooth after the last coat is dry.

Position the pressed side of the fabric over the pattern and lightly trace the pattern onto it in the opposite corners (see pattern placement illustration). Place the fabric in the embroidery hoop.

Use 1 strand of Splendor and the #10 needle to work the curved design areas with closed herringbone stitch (see diagram); the rows on the inside of the curve should be smaller than those on the outside of the curve. Leaves: Use 1 strand of Splendor and satin stitch following the illustration for the stitch direction. Curves: Use 1 strand of Splendor and satin stitch for the curved areas. Whipped spider web: Use 1 strand of Subtlety and the #26 tapestry needle, keeping the web as flat and round as possible. Laid-filling diamond (see diagram): Use 1 strand of Subtlety, coming up at the odd numbers and going down at the even numbers; use 2 strands of Splendor and stem stitch for the outline; use 1 strand of Splendor to tie down the intersections of Subtlety with upright cross stitches.

Remove the fabric from the hoop.

FINISHING

Trim the christening cloth along the pulled-thread lines. Fold the edges to the back ¼ inch (6 mm) on all sides, then fold another ⅛ inch (3 mm) to create a hem. Using 1 strand of Splendor and the crewel needle, and working from the front, hemstitch all the way around the edge, picking up 1/16 inch (1.5 mm) with each stitch. Pull firmly as you stitch and check that you catch the hem at the back of each stitch.

Wash the christening cloth in tepid water and a mild dishwashing liquid. Rinse thoroughly. Roll the cloth in a clean white towel and squeeze gently. Unroll the towel and lay the cloth face down on a padded surface. Straighten the edges and carefully press it. You may spray on a very light coat of starch to give the batiste a little body.

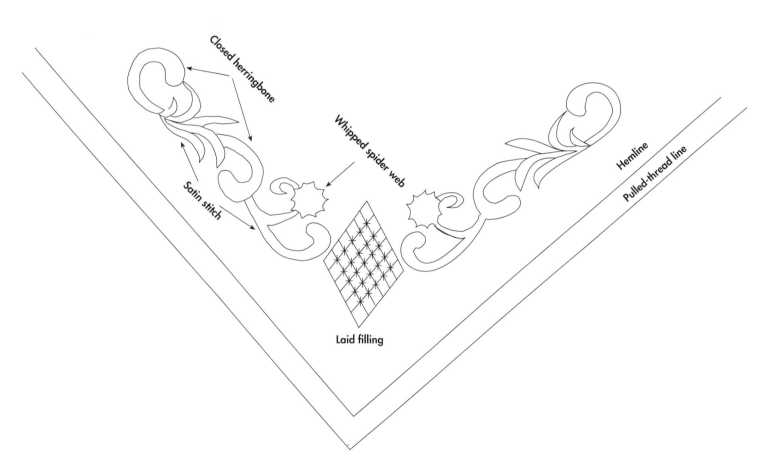

Pattern shown is actual size.
Pattern may be photocopied for personal use.

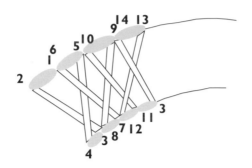

Closed herringbone stitch

Pattern placement

Stitch direction for leaf.

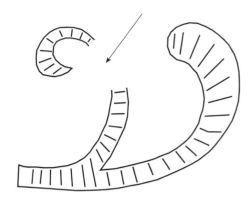

The arrow indicates the placement for the whipped spider web stitch.

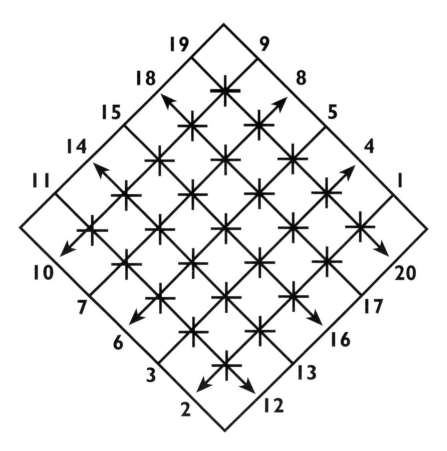

Laid-filling diamond

Needlework for a Good Cause

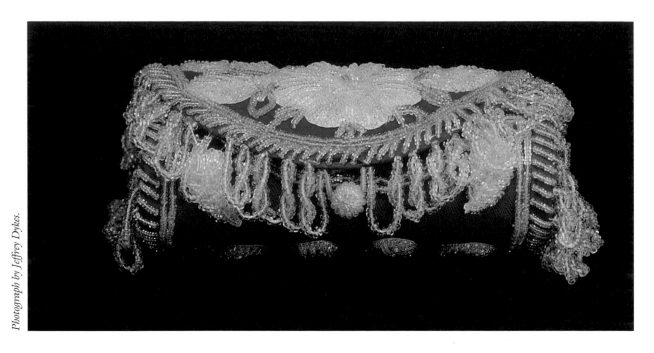

Needle case by Lily P. Kenny. Beads on paper applied to wool; blue silk lining. Salem, Massachusetts. 1862. 5½ × 3 inches (14.0 × 7.6 cm). (130001).

Women always have made use of needlework for artistic expression, to create utilitarian objects, and as a way to spend quiet leisure time. Given the restrictive social conventions of the nineteenth century and the lack of voting rights, some American women of the period also turned to needlework as an outlet for personal expression on public policy. By donating her handwork for sale at a fair or bazaar held to raise money for a worthy cause, a woman could thus participate in certain political activities and social reform movements.

This beaded needle case was made by fourteen-year-old Lily P. Kenny in 1862 and offered for sale at a fund-raiser to benefit Civil War veterans—Lily's father saw active duty with the Massachusetts Volunteer Militia the year Lily made her needle case. The beading technique Lily used emulates that seen in works by Native American bead artists. The use of circular rows at the center of the flowers resembles Native American beaded rosettes, and the petals are done in the lane or lazy stitch, also seen in Native American beading. Clear glass beads against red wool are delicately elegant, but inside the case are an eminently practical pincushion and a pouch for holding small sewing implements.

A NEEDLE BOOK TO EMBROIDER AND BEAD

A NEEDLE BOOK TO EMBROIDER AND BEAD

Needle books make welcome gifts and are an easy-to-make project for a charity bazaar, as was Lily Kenny's original. This red satin one is embellished with seed beads and has a flannel insert to keep needles safe. Needleworkers of all skill levels will enjoy stitching this little case.

MATERIALS

Satin fabric, Red, ½ yard (0.5 meter), cut in half with the grain of the fabric

Interfacing, 1 piece 3⅞ × 7⅞ inches (9.8 × 20.0 cm)

White flannel, 1 piece 3½ × 7 inches (8.9 × 17.8 cm),

Mill Hill Magnifica glass beads, #10009 White, 2 grams

Needles, beading size 12 and sewing (for finishing)

Silamide thread, size A, Black

Sewing thread to match fabric (for finishing) and white (for basting)

Embroidery hoop, 6 inch (15.2 cm)

Pencil, HB

Tissue paper

Finished size: 4 × 4 inches (10.2 × 10.2 cm) folded, 4 × 8 inches (10.2 × 20.3 cm) opened.

INSTRUCTIONS

Trace the pattern and a ½-inch (1.3-cm) seam allowance onto the tissue paper. Center the tissue pattern on the right side of one piece of the satin fabric; pin. Center the fabric in the hoop. Using the sewing needle, baste the tissue onto the fabric with small stitches, following the traced lines. Tear off the tissue. Check the fabric to ensure that the entire design has been stitched.

Use the lazy stitch (see diagram) for all of the beading in the flower and the leaves.

Leaves: Stitch in the long center vein first and tack it down in several places. Add the side stitches starting from the bottom of the leaf (stem end) and working to the top.

Flower: Add the beads in circles starting from the center and working out. When about half the flower is filled with beads, add the straight stitches. Start by stitching in all of the longest and shortest stitches around the flower and then fill in the remaining areas. For the straight stitches along the top of the flower and the base of the stems, use 9 beads for each of the long stems and 6 beads for each of the short stems.

Lower stems: Use beaded feather stitch (see diagram).

Picots: Use 3 beads and stitch along the seam line every ¼ inch (6 mm), making the stitch about the length of 2 beads so that the center bead of the picot pops up.

Remove the fabric from the hoop.

FINISHING

Remove the basting stitches. Apply the interfacing to the wrong side of the beaded fabric according to the manufacturer's directions. Cut the second piece of satin to the same size as the beaded piece to serve as the lining.

Fold the seam allowance of the beaded fabric, to the inside over the interfacing, mitering the corners; tack it down. Fold the seam allowance of the lining to the inside, mitering the corners; pin, and topstitch with matching thread all around 1/8 inch (3 mm) from all edges. Trim the raw edges. Center the piece of flannel on the right side of the lining and anchor along the center line and sew using the white thread. Whipstitch the beaded fabric to the lining along the edges.

Fold

Pattern is shown actual size.
Pattern may be photocopied for personal use.

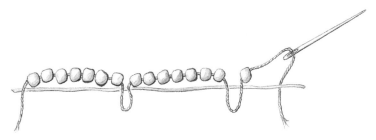

Lazy stitch #1.
Begin by passing the needle through the fabric from wrong side to right side at the place where the first bead is to go. String from 1 to 7 beads, make a stitch in the cloth, string more beads, and repeat.

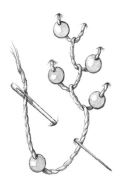

Feather stitch with beads.

Lazy stitch #1 and feather stitch with beads from The Beader's Companion, by Judith Durant and Jean Campbell (Loveland, Colorado: Interweave Press, 1998).

A Cavalier Couple in Beads

Photograph by Jeffrey Dykes.

Panel for a fire screen. Maker unknown. Wool threads and beads on linen. Salem, Massachusetts. 1865–1885. 31½ × 28 inches (80.0 × 71.1 cm). (112921).

The nineteenth century is in its last quarter in Salem, Massachusetts. The Civil War is an immediate memory, the Industrial Revolution in full swing. The nation is rebuilding, men and women are going into factory work in ever-increasing numbers, yet somehow, somewhere, someone takes the time to create this elaborately, laboriously beaded fire screen.

It could be the work of a professional artisan, or of a highly skilled, well-to-do amateur with time to while away in artistic pursuits. In its return to seventeenth-century romantic themes, we see a cavalier courting a lady, a far cry from the real soldiers and real battles of recent years. The literary tastes of that time were influenced by Sir Walter Scott (1771–1832) and Alexandre Dumas (1802–1870), not by later writers such as Stephen Crane (1871–1900).

Fire screens were invented in the early nineteenth century to prevent sparks from flying into the room; and the needlework panel shown here would have been mounted in a frame attached to a base. Open fires were largely a thing of the past in middle- and upper-class households so this late-nineteenth-century example expresses the Victorian impulse for ornamentation. The workmanship is exquisite. Except for the hands and face and, oddly, the lady's purse of peacock feathers, the figures are worked entirely in colored glass beads. These and the background are worked in tent stitch. The panel was part of the furnishings in the Putnam-Balch House on Essex Street in Salem, Massachusetts.

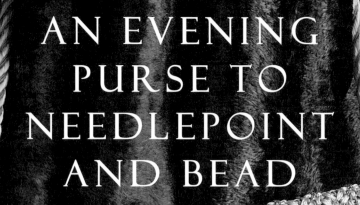

AN EVENING
PURSE TO
NEEDLEPOINT
AND BEAD

AN EVENING PURSE TO NEEDLEPOINT AND BEAD

With the exception of the background, the faces, and the woman figure's peacock purse, the fire-screen panel is stitched with glass beads—a prodigious accomplishment for a piece this large. The peacock purse inspired our bead needlepoint project. The beads are attached to the canvas with a tent stitch. An interesting open pattern makes up the background. We've added a beaded fringe.

MATERIALS

Zweigart 18-count Mono Deluxe Canvas #1282, 100% cotton canvas, Brown #70, 1 piece 18 × 18 inches (45.7 × 45.7 cm)

Satin backing fabric, Ecru, 1 piece 6 x 8 inches (15.2 × 20.3 cm)

Lining fabric, Ecru, 2 pieces 6 × 8 inches (15.2 × 20.3 cm) each

Designing Women Rayon Ribbon Floss, 40 yards (36.5 meters)/spool, #142f-35 Light Moss Green, 1 spool

Designing Women Shimmer Blend Rayon Ribbon Floss, 30 yards (27.4 yards)/spool, #148f-48 Ecru/Gold, 2 spools

Designing Women Reflection Collection Metallic Braid, 15 yards (13.7 meters)/spool, #154-11 Light Gold, 1 spool

DMC Embroidery Floss (Article 117), 100% cotton 6-strand thread, 8.7 yards (8 meters)/skein, 1 skein each in the colors listed in the Color Guide

Mill Hill Beads, 1 packet each in the kinds and colors listed in the Color Guide

Mill Hill Crystal Treasures, in the colors and quantities listed in the Color Guide

Needles, tapestry size 24 (for background),

Page 89: Beaded fringe designed and worked

by Jean Campbell.

beading size 10 (for feather centers) and size 12 for fringe, and sewing (for finishing)

Sewing thread, Ecru

Beading thread, size B Black

Beeswax or thread conditioner

Stretcher frame

Gold cord (for strap), 42 inches (106.7 cm)

Finished size: 7 × 5 inches (17.8 × 12.7 cm)

INSTRUCTIONS

Mount the canvas on the stretcher frame. Use 1 strand of Shimmer Blend for the background and filler stitches. Work the slanted background stitches according to the diagram. You may stitch the bases of the filler stitches as you work the slanted background stitches or after completing all the slanted background stitches. Using a single strand of the Metallic Braid, work the top 2 stitches (indicated as gold on the diagram) on each of the filler stitches. Using tent stitch, work the beaded feather centers with 1 strand of DMC floss (run the floss over the beeswax or thread conditioner for added strength) and a co-ordinating bead (see the Color Key). After applying a row of similarly colored beads, run a long stitch through the row for added stability.

Use 1 strand of DMC Embroidery Floss

#3346 to couch the free-form feather shafts of Designing Women Ribbon Floss. Remove the canvas from the stretcher frame.

FINISHING

Leaving ½ inch (3.8 cm) all around, trim off the excess canvas. Fold under the edges of the canvas so that none shows on the front; clip corners; crease folds. Using the finished front as a template, cut two pieces of lining fabric in the same shape, allowing ½ inch (1.3 cm) for the seams. Cut the backing fabric in the same manner but with a ¾-inch (1.9-cm) seam allowance. Fold under the seam allowance of the backing fabric; pin. With the sewing needle and thread, sew the backing fabric to the back of the purse, leaving the top open. Place the pieces of lining fabric wrong sides together and sew, leaving the top seam open. Trim the seams and clip the corners. Turn the lining wrong side out. Insert the lining into the purse. Attach the gold cord on either side of the purse. Fold the raw edges of the lining outward and whipstitch the edges to the front and backing.

BEADED FRINGE

The chain: Using 36 inches (91.4 cm) of beading thread and leaving a 6-inch (15.2-cm) tail, string 5 Camouflage beads and 1 Periwinkle bead. Pass back through the last Camouflage bead strung so that the Periwinkle bead forms a picot on the string of beads. String 3 Camouflage beads and pass back through the first bead strung. *String 2 Camouflage, 1 Periwinkle, and pass back through the last Camouflage strung to make another picot. String 3 Camouflage and pass back through the second of the last group of 3 Camouflage strung (the third Camouflage from the previous Periwinkle cap). Repeat from * to 3½ inches (8.9 cm). Weave thread through beads so it exits from the last Periwinkle bead added.

The fringe: *String 3 Periwinkle, one 6-mm Treasure, one 4-mm Treasure, and 1 Periwinkle. Pass back through the 4-mm Treasure, the 6-mm Treasure, and the last Periwinkle bead just added. String 2 Periwinkle and pass through the bead on the next Periwinkle point. Weave through the beads on the chain, skipping one Periwinkle point and exiting at the next Periwinkle. Rep from * to the end of the chain. Weave the working and tail threads through several beads to secure and trim close to work.

Work the chain and fringe for the other side of the purse in the same way. Using beading thread, sew to each side of the purse. Add a tassel to the center, if desired

COLOR GUIDE
DMC Embroidery Floss
371—Mustard
3346—Hunter Green
3740—Dark Antique Violet
3842—Dark Wedgwood
3844—Dark Bright Turquoise

Mill Hill
Glass Seed Beads
00206—Violet
Antique Glass Beads

03030—Camouflage
03061—Matte Periwinkle
Magnifica Glass Beads
10029—Brilliant Sage
10079—Brilliant Teal
Crystal Treasures
13088—6mm Amethyst, 16
13070—4mm Olivine, 16

Note: Numbers following the color names refer to the number of Treasures needed.

COLOR KEY

- ■ 00206 Bead and 3740 Floss
- ■ 10029 Bead and 3346 Floss
- ■ 03030 Bead and 371 Floss
- ■ 10079 Bead and 3844 Floss
- ■ 03061 Bead and 3842 Floss

Each line on the diagram represents 1 fabric thread.

Diagram may be photocopied for personal use.

BACKGROUND STITCH

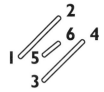

FILLER STITCH 1

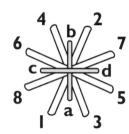

FILLER STITCH 2

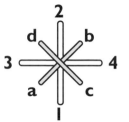

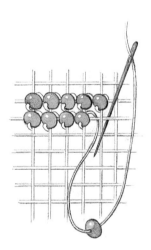

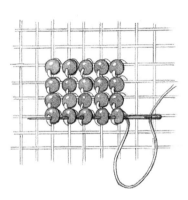

TENT STITCH WITH BEADS

Background stitch adapted from Potpourri of Pattern, by Ann Strite-Kurz (Midland, Michigan: Ann Strite-Kurz, 1995).

Tent stitch with beads from The Beader's Companion, by Judith Durant and Jean Campbell (Loveland, Colorado: Interweave Press, 1998).

Pansies and Roses

Many examples of American needlework throughout history speak not only of the taste and talent of the maker but also of her economic status. A beautifully crafted quilt of homespun broadcloth, for example, would likely have come from a household of lesser means than a similarly crafted quilt of imported silk brocade and velvet.

Women's magazines of the nineteenth century advocated the use of handcrafted upholstery to make furniture more comfortable while demonstrating the family's awareness of culture and prevailing aesthetic tastes. Happily, the materials were within the budget of women of varying economic backgrounds. Berlin woolwork, named for both the soft embroidery wool dyed to brilliant colors in Berlin, Germany, and the hand-painted charts that were published there, was a popular technique boasting widely available materials and patterns as well as a durable product. Many of the Berlin woolwork patterns published during the nineteenth century were based on tapestry designs that had been used in England and continental Europe since the sixteenth century.

The sample of upholstery shown here was probably intended for a chair seat or a seat cushion; it was made between 1865 and 1885. The vivid colors, readily available and taken for granted today, reflect the introduction of aniline dyes during the 1850s.

Photograph by Jeffrey Dykes.

Upholstery fabric. Maker unknown. Wool threads and beads on canvas. Probably Salem, Massachusetts. 1865–1885. 21½ × 22 inches (54.6 × 55.9 cm). (122920).

A FOOTSTOOL
TOP TO
CROSS-STITCH

A FOOTSTOOL TOP TO CROSS-STITCH

The flower motifs worked in tent stitch on the chair seat and embellished with beads are here transposed to the center of the top for a draft footstool. Working the design in a variation of cross-stitch with one strand of wool on canvas produces a durable fabric. Stitching the design in tent stitch on mono canvas with two strands of wool will also be satisfactory.

MATERIALS

Zweigart 13-count Interlock Canvas #604/9604, 100% cotton, 1 piece 18 inches (45.7 cm) square

JCA Paternayan Persian Yarn, 100% wool 3-strand yarn, 8 yards (7.4 meters)/skein, in the colors and amounts listed in the Color Guide

JCA Paternayan Persian Yarn, 100% wool 3-strand yarn, 4 ounces (113.4 g)/hank, 1 hank in the background color, #707 Darkest Green

Needle, tapestry size 22

Sudberry House draft footstool #43001

Finished size: 14 × 14 inches (35.6 × 35.6 cm)

INSTRUCTIONS

Fold the canvas lengthwise, then crosswise to locate the center; mark the center of the canvas.

Begin stitching from the center row, working the stitches from right to left and the rows from the bottom to the top of the canvas. When you have finished working the first half of the design, rotate the canvas and the chart and work the second half in the same way. After the design is worked, continue the background until piece measures finished size.

Using the tapestry needle and 1 strand of yarn throughout, work the cross-stitch variation (see diagram). This cross-stitch variation may be worked on the surface of the canvas with a sewing motion. A frame is unnecessary.

FINISHING

Weave the yarn ends into the back of the work. Mount the canvas onto the footstool according to the manufacturer's directions.

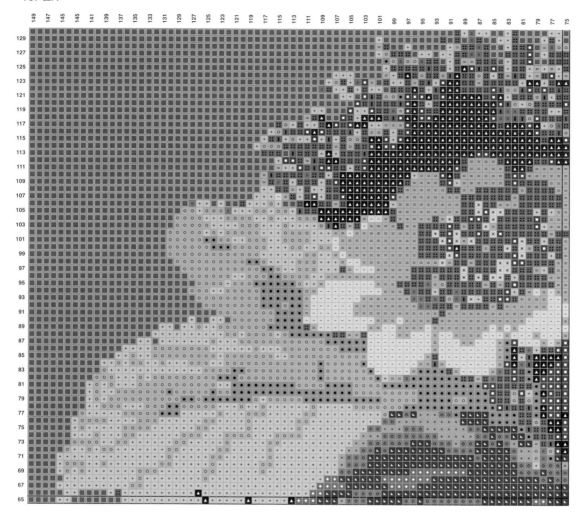

Chart may be photocopied for personal use.
Align charts at duplicate row numbers; duplicate rows are outlined in black.

COLOR GUIDE

▲	220-Black, 2
=	314-Light Grape, 1
▪	320-Dark Plum, 1
∷	321-Medium Plum, 2
−	507-Ice Blue, 1
▮	522-Medium Teal, 1
‖	524-Light Teal, 1
•	662-Dark Pine Green, 1

○	663-Medium Pine Green, 2
+	664-Light Pine Green, 3
✳	701-Butterscotch, 1
▢	707-Darkest Green (background), 1
◣	941-Cranberry, 1
◇	942-Medium Cranberry, 1
×	953-Light Cranberry, 1
◆	967-Dark Red, 1

Note: Numbers following the color names refer to the number of skeins or hanks needed.

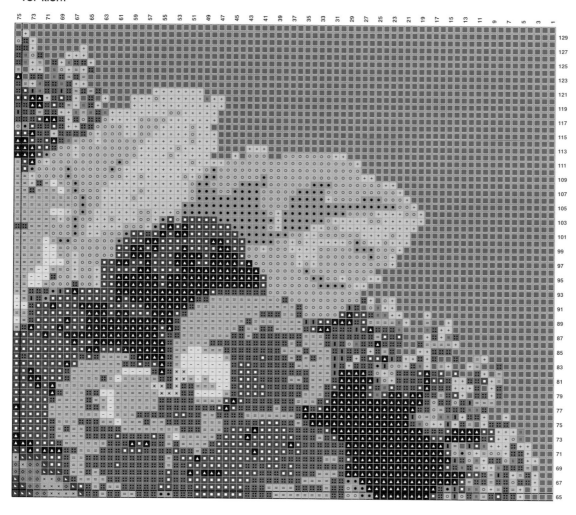

CROSS-STITCH VARIATION.

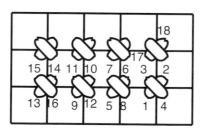

99

A Tasseled Lambrequin

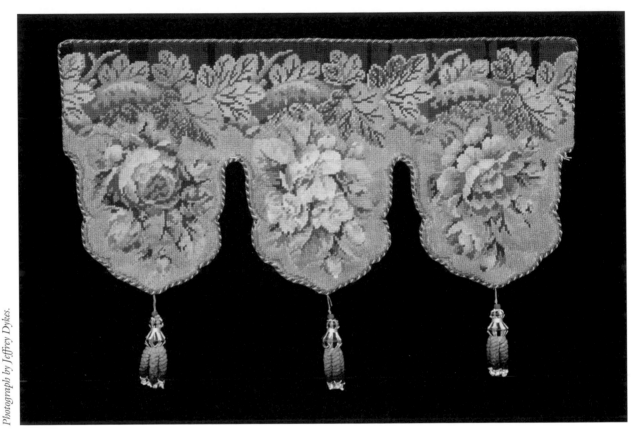

Lambrequin. Maker unknown. Wool threads, silk, and beads on linen. New England.

1875–1885. 14 × 21¼ inches (35.6 × 54.0 cm). (126547).

Throughout the centuries, hundreds of thousands of tassels, small and large, plain and fancy, have been made, using materials ranging from silk and wool to paper, beads, and raffia. Egyptian kings and Genghis Khan wore them; they decorate the outer walls of the Taj Mahal and are carved on monuments. They have adorned pillows, drapery, clothing, bedding, bell pulls, paintings, and jewelry. They were hugely popular during the late nineteenth century.

This lambrequin, or valance, in beaded Berlin woolwork was intended to decorate a windowsill. This needlepoint technique produced a sturdy fabric and was widely used on Victorian-era home furnishings. It is stitched with a leafy vine and three different floral sprays. Iridescent blue-gray glass beads accent the flowers. The stitchery is embellished with three fancy silk tassels. A blue-and-white cord edges the piece.

A TASSEL
TO MAKE

A TASSEL TO MAKE

Silk tassels dangle from the beaded and needlepointed lambrequin that once adorned a mantel, windowsill, or shelf in a fashionable late-nineteenth-century home. This twenty-first-century tassel, made of hand-dyed silk chenille with a copper-colored braid stitched onto the head in detached buttonhole stitch, could serve as a drapery tieback as shown here, decorate a pillow, or be used as drawer or ceiling fan pulls.

MATERIALS

Thread Gatherer Silken Chenille, 100% hand-dyed silk chenille 1-strand thread, 10 yards (9.1 meters)/skein, 2 skeins each of Forest of Greens, Maidenhair Fern, and Vintage Browns

Kreinik Medium (#16) Braid, #215C Antique Copper, 1 reel

Stiff cardboard, 8 × 8 inches (20.3 × 20.3 cm) wide

Needle, tapestry size 20

Heavyweight thread

Copper beads, 6

Finished size: 8 inches (20.3 cm) long

INSTRUCTIONS

Refer to the Stitch Diagrams on pages 116–119. Make a 4-strand braid using 1 strand each of the 3 chenille yarns and 1 strand of the Kreinik Braid (holding the Kreinik Braid with one of the chenille strands). The strands should be cut 2 times the desired finished length of the tieback.

Wrap the cardboard with all three colors of chenille (held together as one strand) about 20 times, 60 total strands. Wrap more strands for a fatter tassel and fewer for a thinner one. Tie the loops together at one end with a strong thread. Slide the threads off the board and, again using the strong thread, tie all the threads together about 1 to 1½ inches (2.5 to 3.8 cm) from the first thread. This will form the neck. Wrap 1 strand of chenille around the neck thread a few times to cover it; secure the ends. Slide the 4-strand braid through the loop made by the first thread. Using the tapestry needle and the Kreinik Braid, work a detached buttonhole stitch around the top of the tassel down to the neck being careful not to catch the 4-strand braid in the stitching. Cut the loops at the bottom of the tassel. Thread the copper beads on random tassel ends and secure with overhand knot.

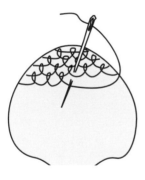

The detached buttonhole stitch is worked around the head of the tassel to add decorative interest. To begin: backstitch a ring around the top of the head of the tassel to serve as an anchor for the buttonhole stitches. Work a row of buttonhole stitches into the backstitch ring and proceed around and down the head until it is covered.

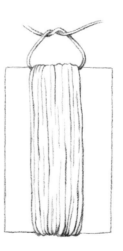

Illustrations from Nicky Epstein's Knitted Embellishments, by Nicky Epstein (Loveland, Colorado: Interweave Press, 1999).

103

Nineteenth-Century Art to Wear

Dress. Maker unknown. Silk threads on wool. American; possibly made of material imported from Europe. Circa 1880. 55 inches (139.7 cm) long. (133939).

Twenty-first-century textile artists use a myriad of materials and techniques to construct what has become known as "art to wear," but creating textiles and clothing as a form of artistic expression is not a new concept. The late nineteenth century saw the proliferation of "art needlework," a style of embroidery that employed free-hand techniques and the skillful use of color shading and varying textures to create a painterly effect.

This dress, stitched about 1880 and believed to have been worn by Mrs. Albert P. Goodhue (1844–1918) of Salem, Massachusetts, would certainly qualify as wearable art by today's standards. The contrast of the glossy silk embroidery with the dark wool ground coupled with the density of the stitches creates motifs that are raised above the surface of the dress. The rose and forget-me-not motifs most likely reflect the "language of flowers," which was so popular during the period. The rose usually represented love or beauty, and the forget-me-not's meaning is proclaimed by its name. It is possible that the embroidery was done by a professional working in England or France and then the embroidered fabric was exported to America; there, its purchaser took it to her dressmaker to be made into a dress.

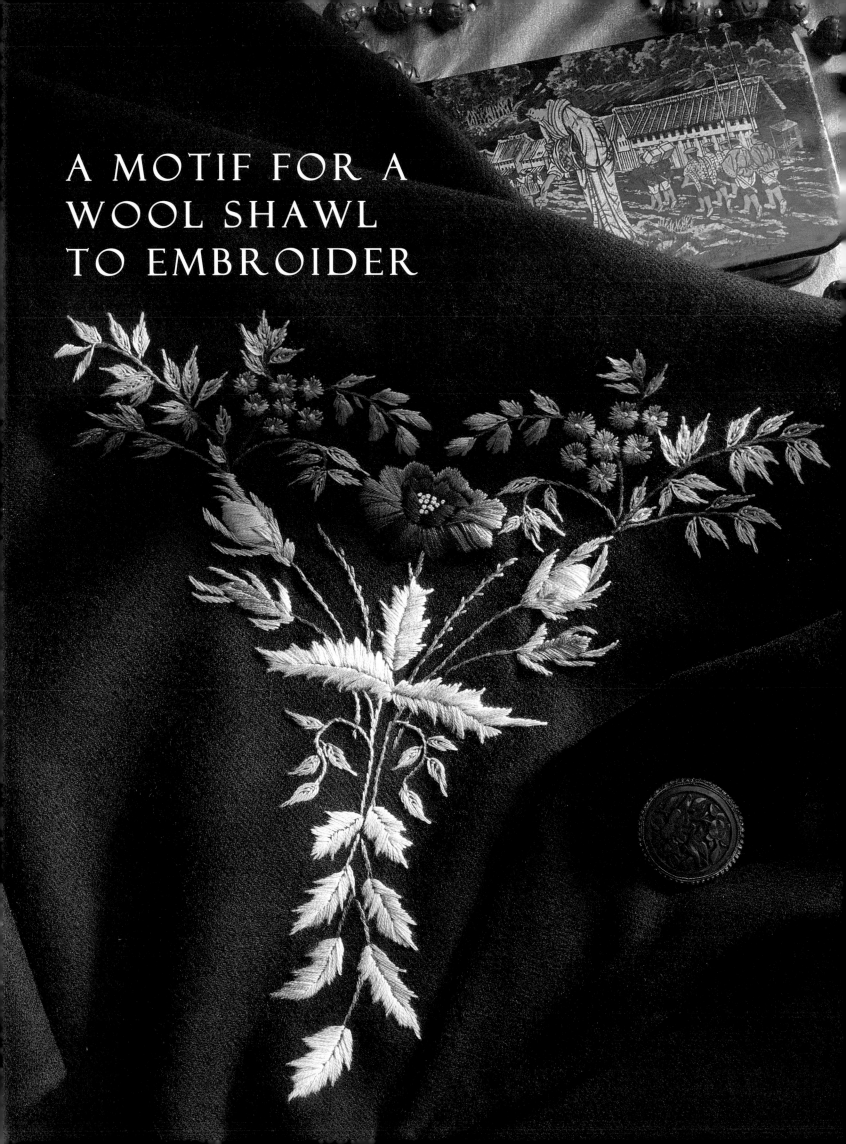

A MOTIF FOR A
WOOL SHAWL
TO EMBROIDER

A MOTIF FOR A WOOL SHAWL TO EMBROIDER

The stunning floral *V* on the back of Mrs. Goodhue's dress was the inspiration for the spray of flowers with one red rose that is the focal point of this V-shaped black wool shawl. The soft Merino wool drapes well; the two ends may be tied in front, or one end may be thrown over the opposite shoulder. Eleven colors of overdyed embroidery floss produce the subtle shading in the flowers, leaves, and stems.

MATERIALS

54-inch (137.2-cm) Merino wool fabric, Black, 2½ yards (2.3 meters)

Needle Necessities Floss Overdyed, 100% cotton 6-strand thread, 20 yards (18.3 meters)/skein, 1 skein each in the colors listed in the Color Guide

Needles, chenille size 24 (for embroidery) and sewing (for basting and finishing)

Sewing thread in a light color (for basting) and black (for finishing)

Embroidery hoop, 8-inch (20.3-cm)

Pencil, HB

Tissue paper

Tailor's chalk

Straightedge

Finished size: Shawl, 53 inches (134.6 cm) deep × 84 inches (213.4 cm) wide; design area, 11½ inches (29.2 cm) high × 11 inches (27.9 cm) wide

INSTRUCTIONS

Refer to Stitch Diagrams on pages 116–119. Fold the fabric in half crosswise and mark the fold with a line of basting using the light-colored sewing thread. This line marks the center back of the shawl. Trace the pattern onto tissue paper. Pin the tissue to the fabric, placing the top of the pattern 12 inches (30.5 cm) down from the raw edge. Again with the light thread, baste the elements of the pattern to the fabric through the tissue. Tear off the tissue. Check to ensure that the entire design has been stitched. Mount the fabric in the hoop.

Using the chenille needle and 2 strands of embroidery floss throughout, work according to the following. Use #1231 and stem stitch for the light stems and stem stitch and #125 for the dark stems. Use #1231 and a small straight stitch for the thorns on the stems below the rose. Use the colors as indicated on pattern and straight and closed fly stitches for leaves. Use #180 and padded satin stitch for the large rosebuds. Use #1571 and straight stitch for the small rosebuds. Use #153 and padded satin stitch for the center of the rose and its front petals. Use #1571 and padded satin stitch for the surrounding petals on the rose. Use #1131 and straight stitch for the blue flowers. Use #162 for the French knots in the center of the blue flower and the red rose. Use #1351 and straight stitch for the blue buds. Remove the fabric from the hoop.

FINISHING

Remove any of the basting threads. Measure and mark with chalk a distance of 42½ inches (108.0 cm) outward from each side of the vertical basting line at the end of the fabric away from the embroidery. With the straightedge and chalk, draw a straight line from each mark to the opposite end of the vertical basting line, forming a *V*. Cut the fabric along the marked lines. Remove any basting stitches. On each raw edge, roll a ½-inch (1.3-cm) hem to the wrong side and stitch in place. Weave the ends of the embroidery floss into the back of the work. Press the shawl using a steam iron and press cloth. Let the fabric cool before removing it from the ironing board.

Page 105: Chinese jewelry and box from the collection

of Martha Lilly, Loveland, Colorado.

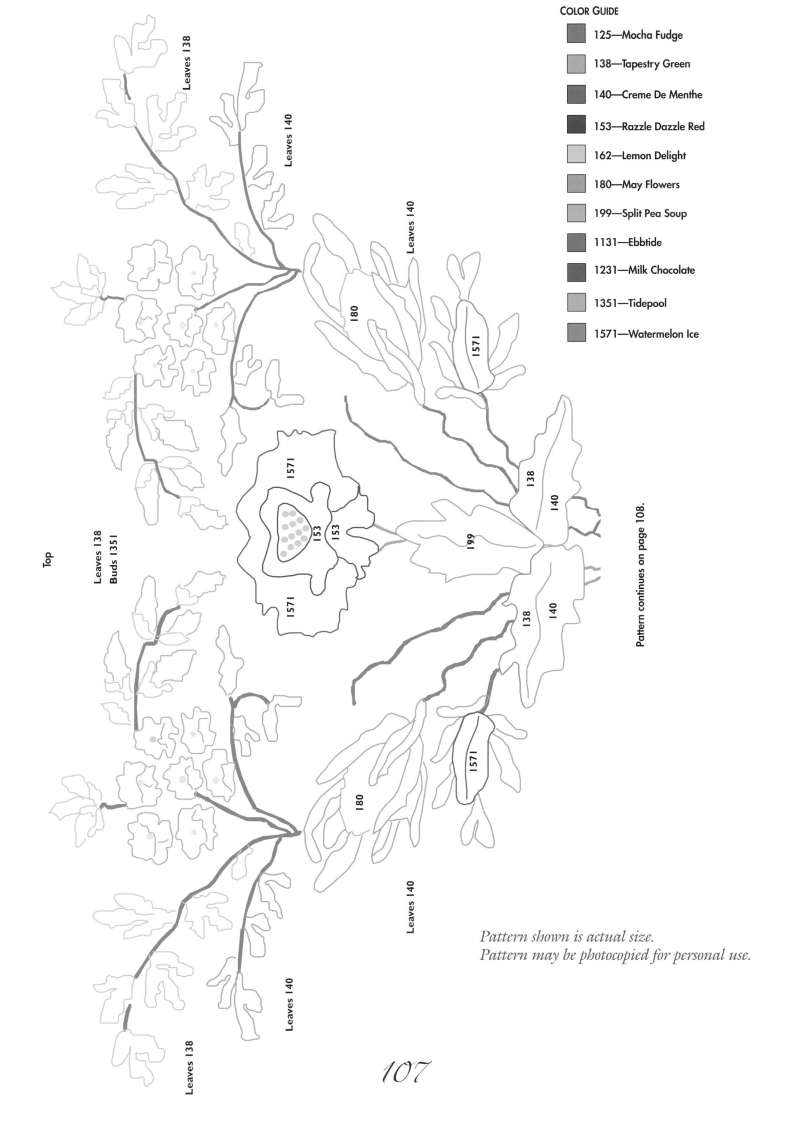

COLOR GUIDE

125—Mocha Fudge
138—Tapestry Green
140—Creme De Menthe
153—Razzle Dazzle Red
162—Lemon Delight
180—May Flowers
199—Split Pea Soup
1131—Ebbtide
1231—Milk Chocolate
1351—Tidepool
1571—Watermelon Ice

Leaves 138
Leaves 140
Leaves 140
180
1571
1571
153   153
1571
1571
199
138
140
138
140
180
1571
Leaves 140
Top
Leaves 138
Buds 1351
Leaves 140
Leaves 138

Pattern continues on page 108.

Pattern shown is actual size.
Pattern may be photocopied for personal use.

107

COLOR GUIDE

■	125—Mocha Fudge
■	138—Tapestry Green
■	140—Creme De Menthe
■	153—Razzle Dazzle Red
■	162—Lemon Delight
■	180—May Flowers
■	199—Split Pea Soup
■	1131—Ebbtide
■	1231—Milk Chocolate
■	1351—Tidepool
■	1571—Watermelon Ice

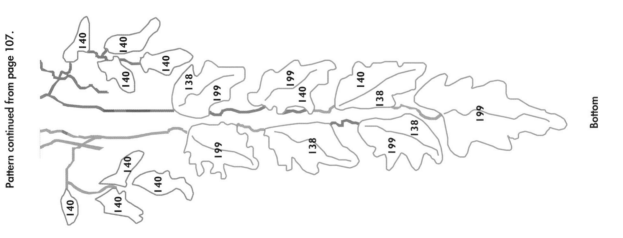

Pattern continued from page 107.

Bottom

Pattern shown is actual size.
Pattern may be photocopied for personal use.

A LID FOR A CRYSTAL JAR TO EMBROIDER

A LID FOR A CRYSTAL JAR TO EMBROIDER

Pink and red roses and forget-me-nots are the floral motifs embroidered on Mrs. Goodhue's dark green wool dress (on page 104). One of the pink roses is featured on the cover of this book. One pink rose on black silk fabric is the centerpiece of the crystal jar lid. The design is worked in a combination of long-and-short and satin stitches with slight padding in the rose and the two buds.

MATERIALS

Slubbed silk fabric, Black, 1 piece, 8 x 8 inches (20.3 × 20.3 cm)

Caron Collection Waterlilies, 100% hand-painted silk 12-strand thread, 6 yards (5.5 meters)/skein, 1 skein each in the colors listed in the Color Guide

Kreinik Silk Mori, 100% silk 6-strand thread, 2.5 meters/skein, 1 skein each in the colors listed in the Color Guide

Needles, betweens size 9 (for embroidery) and sewing (for basting)

Basting thread

Embroidery hoop, 6-inch (15.2-cm)

Tissue paper

Anne Brinkley Designs crystal jar, #CT4

Finished size: 3½ inches (8.9 cm) in diameter

INSTRUCTIONS

Refer to Stitch Diagrams on pages 116–119. Trace the pattern (omitting the outer circle) onto the tissue paper. Center the tissue pattern on the fabric. Center the fabric in the hoop. Using the sewing needle and sewing thread, baste the tissue to the fabric with small stitches, following the traced lines. Tear off the tissue. Check the fabric to ensure that entire design has been stitched.

Using the betweens needle, work the stitches in the direction shown on the pattern and as indicated below.

Flower petals: Use long-and-short, padded satin, or satin stitch and 2 strands of Silk Mori #3011 for light areas and #1103 for dark areas.

Stamens: Use French knots and 3 strands of Silk Mori #2024.

Stems: Use stem stitch and 4 strands of Waterlilies #137.

Leaves: Use satin stitch and 3 strands of Waterlilies #089.

Buds: Use padded satin stitch and 3 strands of Silk Mori #3011 for the upper part of each bud; use #1103 for the lower part.

Remove the fabric from the hoop.

FINISHING

Remove any of the basting stitches. Weave the thread ends into the back of the work. Trim off excess fabric. Center the design and mount in the lid according to the supplier's directions.

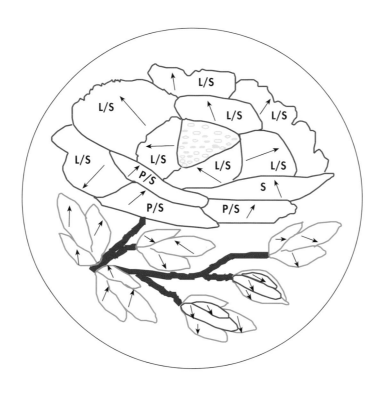

COLOR GUIDE

Waterlilies
089—Caribbean

137—Copper

Silk Mori
1103—Light Mauve

2024—Medium Buttercup

3011—Very Pale Coral

Pattern may be photocopied for personal use.

A Cape in the Arts and Crafts Style

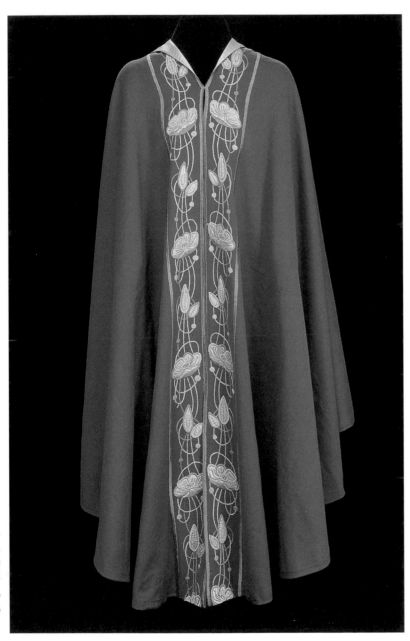

Liberty of London woman's evening cape. Maker unknown.

Silk embroidery and appliqué on wool. England. 1900–1905.

65 inches (165.1 cm) long. (137950).

Stained glass, bronze sculpture, fabric prints, furniture, architecture, and needlework all were greatly influenced by the Arts and Crafts movement of the late nineteenth and early twentieth centuries. In England, William Morris (1834–1896) created what would become one of the most important home decorating collections of all time. In America, Louis Comfort Tiffany (1848-1933) specialized in glasswork. In 1875, Arthur Lasenby Liberty (1843–1917) founded Liberty of London, a retail firm that commissioned the work of leading Arts and Crafts designers. Throughout England and America, needleworkers embroidered the period's decorative motifs onto curtains, pillows, towels, table linens, and clothing. Even today, many artists and designers, especially interior designers, continue to be influenced by the Arts and Crafts style.

The embroidered and appliquéd floral design embellishing the opening of this graceful Liberty of London evening cape is immediately recognizable as being in the Arts and Crafts style. The semicircular pink wool cape is in the form of a medieval liturgical garment. Mrs. Charles Storrow (1858–1943) of Brookline, Massachusetts, purchased the cape in the first years of the twentieth century.

A TABLE
RUNNER TO
EMBROIDER

A TABLE RUNNER TO EMBROIDER

Circles of vines, blossoms, and leaves stitched with silk thread embellish this beautiful linen table runner. The motif, taken from the edges of the Liberty of London wool-and-silk evening cape, is worked in stem and satin stitches and French knots. It is mirrored on either side of a central cluster of leaves; the entire design measures 55 inches (139.7 cm) long. Smaller elements of the motif would make a lovely edging for placemats, napkins, or pillowcases.

MATERIALS

Access Commodities Ecclesiastical Linen, 100% linen, Bright White #FBR10100, 1 piece, 59 × 24 inches (149.9 × 61.0 cm)

Rainbow Gallery Elegance, 100% twisted silk Pearl #8 nondivisible thread, 20 yards (18.2 m)/card, 4 cards each Antique Mauve #E824 and Dark Antique Mauve #E825

Embroidery hoop, 12-inch (30.5-cm) oval

Needles, crewel size 5 (for embroidery) and sewing (for hem)

Matching thread (for finishing)

Pencil, HB

Tissue paper

Finished size: 58 × 23 inches (147.3 × 58.4 cm); design size, 55 × 8 inches (139.7 × 20.3 cm)

INSTRUCTIONS

Refer to the Stitch Diagrams on pages 116–119. The design consists of a central leaf-cluster motif with mirror-image flowers and vines on either side. The reduced line drawing shows the entire motif. Trace the pattern onto the tissue paper. Center the tissue pattern on the right side of the fabric; pin. Using the sewing needle, baste the tissue onto the fabric with small stitches, following the traced lines. Tear off the tissue. Check the fabric to ensure that the entire design has been stitched. Mount the fabric in the hoop.

Follow the patterns for inch measurements, color, and placement. Stitch with 1 strand of thread throughout.

Leaves: Use satin stitch for the outlines; use stem stitch for the inner lines.

Flowers: Use satin stitch for the outlines and dark inner areas; use stem stitch for the inner lines; use French knots for the centers.

Connecting cords and balls: Use satin stitch.

FINISHING

Fold a ½-inch (1.3-cm) hem to the wrong side, then fold to ¼ inch (6 mm). Using the sewing needle and matching thread, hem all edges.

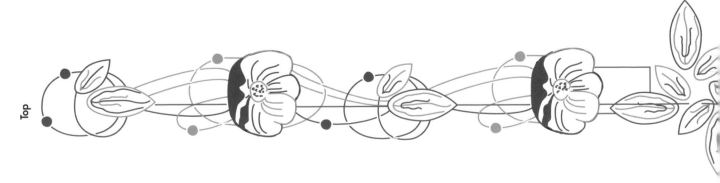

Top

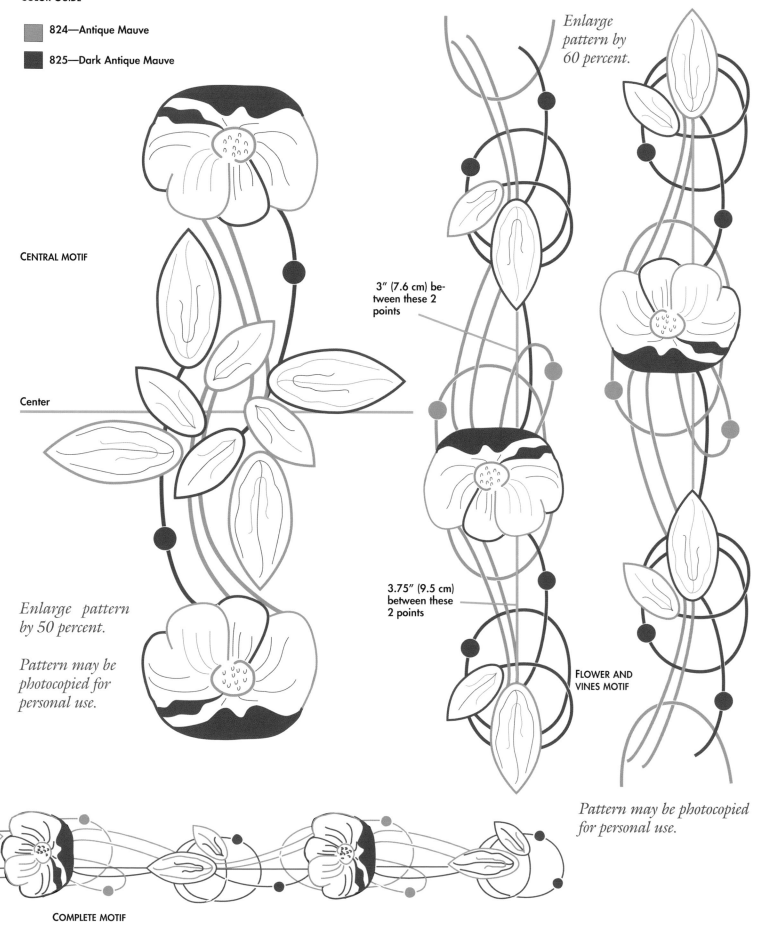

COLOR GUIDE

824—Antique Mauve

825—Dark Antique Mauve

CENTRAL MOTIF

Center

Enlarge pattern by 50 percent.

Pattern may be photocopied for personal use.

Enlarge pattern by 60 percent.

3″ (7.6 cm) between these 2 points

3.75″ (9.5 cm) between these 2 points

FLOWER AND VINES MOTIF

Pattern may be photocopied for personal use.

COMPLETE MOTIF

Stitch Diagrams

These stitch diagrams are for stitches included in multiple projects. The diagrams for stitches that pertain to only one project are with the instructions for that project. Some diagrams are numbered to indicate that the needle comes to the surface at the odd numbers and to the back at the even numbers. In some diagrams, arrows are substituted for numbers to indicate the direction of the stitches.

ALTERNATING OBLONG CROSS-STITCH

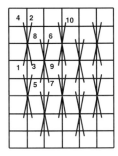

BACK STITCH

This stitch is frequently used to outline motifs.

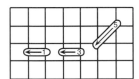

BASKETWEAVE STITCH

Basketweave stitches are worked in diagonal rows (Figure 1) according to the weave of the canvas (Figure 2). The stitches in the descending rows are worked over canvas intersections

Stitch diagrams provided by Kaz Designs, Reston, Virginia.

where the top canvas thread is running in a vertical position. The stitches in the ascending rows are worked over canvas intersections where the top canvas thread runs horizontally.

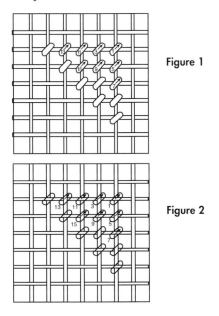

Figure 1

Figure 2

BULLION KNOT STITCH

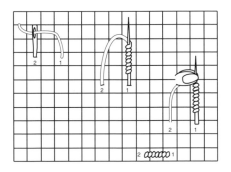

BUTTONHOLE STITCH

The buttonhole stitch may be worked in a line, a circle, or on the outer edges of a kloster block. Begin by bringing the needle to the front of the embroidery (Figure 1) at 1 and inserting it at 2. Keeping the thread loop below the needle, insert the needle again at 3. Continue working as shown in Figure 2. A small stitch is worked over the last loop (Figure 3).

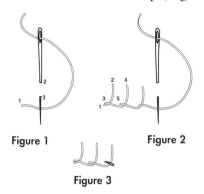

Figure 1   **Figure 2**

Figure 3

CLOSED FLY STITCH

Come up at 1 (Figure 1) and down at 2. Emerge again at 3, loop the yarn as if making a chain stitch, go down at 4, and up at 5 (same hole as 2). Work a tacking stitch (Figure 2). Continue placing stitches next to each other so that no fabric is showing. Tack stitches should share holes to give each fly stitch a proper slant.

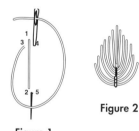

Figure 1   **Figure 2**

COUCHING

Threads may be applied to the surface of the work by means of small couching stitches at regular intervals. Couching may be done in straight, regular intervals, or it may be done around curves.

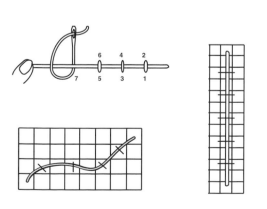

CROSS-STITCH OVER 1 THREAD

CROSS-STITCH OVER 2 THREADS

DETACHED CHAIN STITCH

This stitch is also known as the lazy daisy stitch. The stitches are individual stitches that begin and end in the same hole. Each stitch is secured by a tie-down stitch. Come up at 1 and down at 2. While holding the thread in a loop, take a small stitch at 3–4 to secure the stitch in the desired direction. These stitches may be worked in any direction and may be of any size.

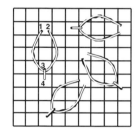

DIAMOND RAY STITCH

Work the units of the ray stitch from the top row to the bottom row.

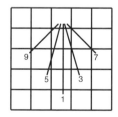
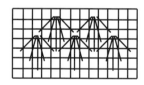

DIRECTIONAL ENCROACHING GOBELIN

The stitches may be slanted in any direction based on the design element..

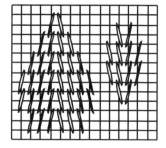

DOUBLE CROSS-STITCH

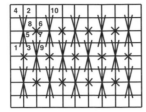

ENCROACHING GOBELIN

The stitches interlock or overlap with the rows above and below.

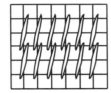

FEATHER STITCH

Feather stitch is easiest worked from the top down. Bring the needle to the surface at 1, hold the thread with the thumb and insert the needle again at 2. Come out again at 3, below and to the left of 2.

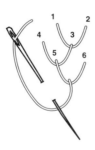

FLY STITCH

This is an open-loop stitch with a short tie-down stitch. Begin at one, hold the thread down with the thumb and insert the needle at 2, coming out below at 3. Pull the thread through at 3 to form the tie-down stitch ending at 4. The fly stitch is basically a detached chain stitch with the loop open rather than closed.

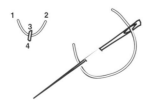

FRENCH KNOT

Hold the thread between your body and the needle and wrap once or twice before going back into the fabric or canvas in a hole adjacent to the one in which the knot was started. When stitching clusters of French knots, you may wish to overlap the knots to build up height.

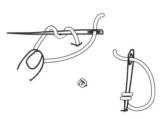

LONG-AND-SHORT STITCH

Long-and-short stitches may be of regular or irregular lengths and should pierce the stitches above to achieve a realistic effect.

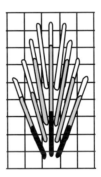

NEEDLEWEAVING

Make 2 long stitches (1–2 and 3–4). Come back up again at 2 and wrap over and under. Continue wrapping until the area between the long stitches is filled. Keep the wraps next to each other; do not twist.

PADDED SATIN STITCH

Padded satin stitches are made by laying a bottom row of stitches with a shape (Figure 1), then covering them with slanted stitches (Figure 2) or stitches that are perpendicular to the bottom layer.

Figure 1　　　**Figure 2**

RANDOM RAY STITCH

Random ray stitches may be stitched any size and make good leaves. Straight stitches may be inserted where needed.

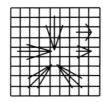

RANDOM SPLIT GOBELIN

The stitches are worked in random lengths and intervals and pierce the stitches in the row above.

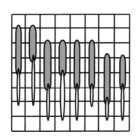

SATIN STITCH

Satin stitches may be straight (Figure 1) or slanted (Figure 2) to suit the space and design requirements.

Figure 1　　　**Figure 2**

SPIDER WEB

Stitch the spokes first (indicated by numbers and arrows). Bring the thread back to the surface and weave forward over 2 spokes and back 1. Fill the area created by the spokes with the weaving.

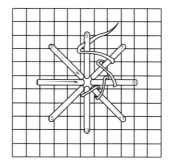

STEM STITCH

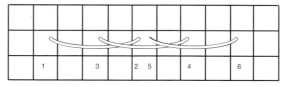

TENT STITCH

Tent stitches are small diagonal stitches slanting from the lower left to the upper right. When worked in rows from right to left or top to bottom, they are called Continental stitches. When worked in diagonal rows, they are called basketweave stitches.

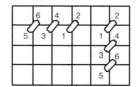

TWISTED CHAIN STITCH

Come up at 1 and form a loop. Go down at 2 and take a small stitch to 3 while bringing the tip of the needle over the thread (Figure 1). Repeat for as long as desired (Figure 2), and end with a small stitch at the end (Figure 3).

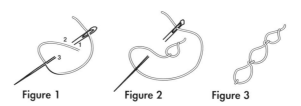

Figure 1　　　**Figure 2**　　　**Figure 3**

119

Suppliers

FABRICS

Access Commodities. (972) 563-3313. Call for the name of your nearest retailer.

Capitol Imports. (850) 385-4665. Call for the name of your nearest retailer.

Wichelt Imports, Inc., N162 Hwy. 35, Stoddard, WI 54658-9711. Visit your local needlework store or order from Needle Arts Services, PO Box 2122, La Crosse, WI 54602-2122.

Zweigart Fabrics, 2 Riverview Dr., Somerset, NJ 08873-1139. (732) 271-1949. Call or write for the name of your nearest retailer.

THREADS AND YARNS

The Caron Collection, 55 Old South Ave., Stratford, CT 06615. (203) 381-9999; www.caron-net.com. Contact Caron for the name of your nearest retailer.

DMC Corp., South Hackensack Ave., Port Kearny Bldg. 10A, South Kearny, NJ 07032. Visit your local needlework store or order from Herrschners. (800) 441-0838; www.herrschners.com.

Designing Women, 601 Champagnolle, El Dorado, AR 71730. (870) 862-0021. Call or write for the name of your nearest retailer.

Gumnut Yarns, Custom House of Needle Arts, 154 Weir St., Glastonbury, CT 06033. (860) 633-2950. Call or write for the name of your nearest retailer.

JCA, Inc., 35 Scales Ln., Townsend, MA 01469-1094. (978) 597-8794. Call or write for the name of your nearest retailer.

JL Walsh Silk, 4338 Edgewood, Oakland, CA 94602. (510) 530-7343. Call or write for the name of your nearest retailer.

Kreinik Mfg. Co., Inc., 3106 Timanus Lane, Ste. 101, Baltimore, MD 21244. (410) 281-0040; www.kreinik.com; e-mail kreinik@kreinik.com. Contact Kreinik for the name of your nearest retailer.

Needle Necessities Inc., 7211 Garden Grove Blvd., #B/C, Garden Grove, CA 92841. (714) 892-9211; www.needlenecessities.com. Contact Needle Necessities for the name of your nearest retailer.

Rainbow Gallery, 7412 Fulton Ave., #5, N. Hollywood, CA 91605. www.rainbowgallery.com. Visit your local needlework store.

The Thread Gatherer, 2108 Norcrest Dr., Boise, ID 83705. (208) 387-2641; e-mail Threadgath@aol.com. Contact the Thread Gatherer for the name of your nearest retailer.

ACCESSORIES, CRYSTAL

Anne Brinkley Designs, Inc., 3895-B N Oracle Rd., Tucson, AZ 85705-3252. (520) 888-1462; e-mail annebrinkleydes @aol.com. Contact Anne Brinkley Designs for the name of your nearest retailer.

ACCESSORIES, METAL

Wichelt Imports, Inc., N162 Hwy. 35, Stoddard, WI 54658-9711. Visit your local needlework store or order from Needle Arts Services, PO Box 2122, La Crosse, WI 54602-2122.

ACCESSORIES, WOODEN

Sudberry House, PO Box 895, Old Lyme, CT 06371. (860) 739-6951; www.sudberry.com. Contact Sudberry House for the name of your nearest retailer.

BEADS

Mill Hill. (608) 754-9466; fax (608) 754-0665; www.millhill.com. Contact Mill Hill for the name of your nearest retailer.

SJ Designs, 1542 Aberdeen St., Chicago Heights, IL 60411. (708) 754-7657. Contact SJ Designs for the name of your nearest retailer.

MISCELLANEOUS NEEDLEWORK SUPPLIES

Needles, stretcher frames, embroidery hoops, perforated paper, finishing services, etc., are available at needlework stores.

MISCELLANEOUS SEWING SUPPLIES

Sewing threads, Velcro or snap fasteners, ribbon, silk, wool, and satin fabrics, tailor's chalk, interfacing, Dritz Cover Button Kit, muslin, etc., are available at fabric stores.

MISCELLANEOUS BEADING SUPPLIES

Silamide thread, beading needles, etc., are available at beading stores.

OTHER SUPPLIES

Pillar candle, pillowcases, potpourri, chiffon scarf, etc., are available at department and craft stores.

Resources

NEEDLEWORK ORGANIZATIONS
American Needlepoint Guild, Inc.
ANG, Inc., Membership Office
PO Box 1027
Cordova, TN 38088-1027
(901) 755-3728; fax:(901) 755-3803
E-mail: Membership@needlepoint.org
Website: www.needlepoint.org

Embroiderers' Guild of America, Inc.
EGA National Headquarters
335 West Broadway, Ste. 100
Louisville, KY 40202-2105
(502) 589-6956; fax: (502) 584-7900
E-mail: EGAHQ@aol.com
Website: www.egausa.org

MUSEUM
Peabody Essex Museum
East India Square
Salem, MA 01970-3783
(978) 745-9500; fax: (978) 744-6776
E-mail: pem@pem.org
Website: www.pem.org

BIBLIOGRAPHY

Ashelford, Jane. *The Art of Dress: Clothes and Society, 1500– 1914.* New York: Abrams, 1996.

Beck, S. William. *Gloves, Their Annals and Associations.* 1883. Reprint, Detroit: Singing Tree Press, 1969.

Beck, Thomasina. *The Embroiderer's Story.* Newton Abbot, Devon, England: David and Charles, 1995.

———-. *Gardening with Silk and Gold: A History of Gardens in Embroidery.* Newton Abbot, Devon, England: David and Charles, 1977.

Bolton, Ethel Stanwood, and Eva Johnston Coe. *American Samplers.* New York: Dover, 1973.

Caulfeild, Sophia Frances Anne, and Blanche C. Saward. *The Dictionary of Needlework: An Encyclopaedia of Artistic, Plain and Fancy Needlework.* 1882. Reprint, New York: Arno Press, 1972.

Durant, Judith, and Jean Campbell. *The Beader's Companion.* Loveland, Colorado: Interweave Press, 1998.

Epstein, Kathleen. *British Embroidery: Curious Works from the Seventeenth Century.* Austin, Texas: Curious Works Press, 1998.

Harbeson, Georgiana Brown. *American Needlework: The History of Decorative Stitchery and Embroidery from the Late 16th to the 20th Century.* New York: Bonanza Books, 1938.

Huish, Marcus B. *Samplers and Tapestry Embroideries.* 1900. Reprint, New York: Dover, 1970.

Humphrey, Carol. *Samplers: Fitzwilliam Museum Handbook.* Cambridge, England: Cambridge University Press, 1997.

Krueger, Glee. *New England Samplers to 1840.* Sturbridge, Massachusetts: Old Sturbridge Village, 1978.

Levey, Santina M. *Discovering Embroidery of the Nineteenth Century.* Aylesbury, Buckinghamshire, England: Shire, 1977.

Morris, Barbara. *Victorian Embroidery.* New York: Nelson, 1962.

Paine, Sheila. *Embroidered Textiles: Traditional Patterns from Five Continents.* New York: Thames and Hudson, 1990.

Parker, Rozsika. *The Subversive Stitch: Embroidery and the Making of the Feminine.* London: Routledge, Kegan and Paul, 1989.

Parry, Linda. *Textiles of the Arts and Crafts Movement.* New York: Thames and Hudson, 1988.

———. *William Morris Textiles.* New York: Crescent Books, 1983.

Ring, Betty. *American Needlework Treasures.* New York: Dutton, 1990.

———. *Girlhood Embroidery: American Samplers and Pictorial Needlework, 1650–1850.* New York: Knopf, 1993.

Scoble, Gretchen, and Ann Field. *The Meaning of Flowers: Myth, Language and Lore.* San Francisco: Chronicle Books, 1998.

Serena, Raffaella. *Berlin Work, Samplers and Embroidery of the Nineteenth Century.* Berkeley, California: Lacis, 1996.

Swan, Susan Burrows. *Plain and Fancy: American Women and Their Needlework, 1650–1850.* Austin, Texas: Curious Works Press, 1995.

Welch, Nancy. *Tassels: The Fanciful Embellishment.* Asheville, North Carolina: Lark Books, 1997.

Index